SIGNS TO THE END OF THIS AGE

by

Joseph S. Houlahan

ELI PRESS

121, Low Etherley, Bishop Auckland, Co. Durham, DL14 0HA

2011

ISBN 978-1-908788-01-6

Printed by

ELI PRESS
121, Low Etherley, Bishop Auckland,
Co. Durham, DL14 0HA

Acknowledgements

First and foremost I would like to thank my Lord and Savior, Jesus Christ. He called me and gave me the desire and passion to study the book of Revelation and his second coming. The lord has given me strength and patience to persevere despite much opposition from the enemy.

I would like to thank Iris Ferguson (my wife's friend for almost 60 years) for typing my notes.

My oldest son Colin for spending many hours proof reading.

My granddaughter Devon for editing the book.

Andrew and Alison Briton for their technical support.

Jim Robinson who gave me the contact details for the publisher.

Last but not least my youngest son Mark who encouraged me to turn my years of studying into a book and who supported me during this process.

Thanks again to everyone who has helped.

Joseph S. Houlahan

Dedication

In June 2012, God willing, I would have been married to my dear wife for 50 years. I would like to dedicate this book to Ruth for her endurance and her patience with me as I have studied 3-4 hours most days for over 30 years. Throughout this time she has shown love and commitment to me and our family, without her support I would never have been able to produce this book. I love you Ruth.

Just a few months, after celebrating our 50th wedding anniversary, Ruth went to be with the Lord. Then God took me into Matthew chapter 24, and in the last 8 months he revealed to me a greater understanding of the future. What he revealed to me is that both Matthew 24 and Revelation have identical ending of Christ's second coming.

I have written this for you to read before reading my book. It will help you to gain a greater understanding of the truth, which, is so perfectly revealed of what is going to happen in the last 3½ years.

I pray you may receive the same revelation that I received from the Lord.

MATTHEW CHAPTER 24

A REDUCING TIME SCALE TO THE SECOND COMING OF JESUS CHRIST

Verse 1 Jesus Christ was departing from the Temple in Jerusalem. His disciples were showing and admiring the structure of it. Little did they realise that the Lord was going to speak of a descaling of events of generations, to the second coming of the Lord.

Verse 2 JESUS FIRST FORETELLS THE DESTRUCTION OF THE TEMPLE.

"DO YOU NOT SEE ALL THESE THINGS? ASSUREDLY, I SAY TO YOU, "NOT ONE STONE SHALL BE LEFT HERE UPON ANOTHER THAT SHALL NOT BE THROWN DOWN."

This proves that Jesus Christ knows the future, for this event happened 40 years after the death and resurrection of Christ. In Revelation chapter 1 verse 17 Jesus said "Do not be afraid, I am the first and the last, I am he that liveth and was dead and behold I am alive for evermore, Amen." He even said, when speaking, "Before Abraham, was I am", so our Lord knew everything from the beginning of creation to the end of creation. So our Lord was telling them of the destruction of this temple. Jesus foretold in this chapter of many Prophecies as we shall read through this Chapter.

THE NEED FOR DISCIPLES TO ASK AND SEEK FOR FUTURE EVENTS TO JESUS CHRIST'S SECOND COMING

Verse 3 THE DISCIPLES CAME TO HIM PRIVATELY, SAYING, "TELL US WHEN WILL THESE THINGS BE? AND WHAT WILL BE THE SIGN OF YOUR COMING AND THE END OF THE AGE?"

As disciples of Christ we must seek as it is very important to ask and find the time of Jesus Christ's second coming and of the end of the age. For we read in the next verses many deceivers will come to confuse believers regarding his second coming. It is of the utmost importance we hear God's Son for this truth.

THEN CAME THE WARNING OF DECEPTION TO THE TRUTH OF JESUS CHRIST

Verse 4 TAKE HEED THAT NO ONE DECEIVES YOU FOR MANY WILL COME IN MY NAME, SAYING "I AM CHRIST" AND WILL DECEIVE MANY.

Satan has deceived himself to think he is a God who also is the deceiver of the world, and seeks everyone to worship him. When tempting Jesus Christ he said, "All these things will I give you if you will bow down and worship me." The Bible has declared that we have all been deceived by him for we have all sinned and come short of the standard for heaven. But Jesus said to him, "Away with you Satan, for it is written you shall worship the Lord thy God and him only you shall serve."

So Satan is the God of deception in the world today. Even Israel, a nation, God raised up to be his chosen people was also deceived. As we read in the Old Testament how they went to worship the idols of other gods in the Nations around them. Despite this, God sent his Son Jesus Christ to be the Saviour of the world, and by his death and resurrection and his ascension into Heaven so that whosoever repent of their sins has eternal life. This is the faith of every believer. But the world has been deceived by Satan who has created in the mind of nearly every person to worship idols in every nation or have looked upon emperors as Kings and gods in their countries. So Satan is the deceiver of every country throughout the world.

IN MATTHEW CHAPTER 24 CHRIST FORETELLS A REDUCING TIME SCALE TO HIS SECOND COMING

SATAN HAS THE POWER TO CREATE ALL WARS.

Verse 6 AND YOU WILL HEAR OF WARS AND RUMOURS OF WARS SEE THAT YE ARE NOT TROUBLED FOR ALL THESE TIHINGS MUST COME TO PASS BUT THE END IS NOT YET (EVIDENCE OF WARS, IN JOB).

In the book of Job Chapter 1 and 2 Satan is allowed by God to try the faith of Job. We read how he brought two nations. The Sabean and the Chaldeans to attack Job. After he received blessing from God by making him one of the richest men of his day. Satan took all his wealth away and used wind and fire against his family and sheep, and left him with only his wife alive. Then he attacked his body nearly unto death and his faith was tried to the limit, but his integrity stood firm with God. Satan was the one who brought two nations against Job, and Job was a descendant of Noah, after God destroyed the world's population because every imagination of people's hearts were evil. The trials of our faith are more precious than gold, though it be tried by fire (like Job). Therefore wars were from Satan from 6000 years ago until the present time. Every nation in the world has a history of wars from generation to generation. History books proves every nation has a history of wars from years ago.

HOW GOD'S REDUCING TIME SCALE DROPPED TO 100 YEARS

Verse 7 FOR NATION WILL RISE AGAINST NATION, AND KINGDON AGAINST KINGDOM THERE WILL BE FAMINES, PESTILENCES AND EARTHQUAKES IN VARIOUS PLACES.

In this one verse, we see a drop in the times scale from 6000 years to one hundred years then to fifty years.

Then kingdom against kingdom.

In the last hundred years there has been two World Wars.

1st from – 1914 to 1918 (1st kingdom against kingdom)
2nd from – 1939 to 1945 (2nd kingdom against kingdom)

After two world wars the time scale dropped to fifty years as we have seen on world news of famines, pestilences and earthquakes in many nations of the world. This has affected millions of people.

Verse 8 ALL THESE ARE THE BEGINNING OF SORROWS.

Our Lord spoke of this as a great time of sorrow in the earth.

IN THE LAST FIFTY YEARS THESE THREE TERRIBLE EVENTS FAMINES, PESTILENCES AND EARTHQUAKES.

As we consider these three world evil disasters that has struck parts of the nations of the world, we see the intensity of Satan's evil power upon the world. As the end draws near when God will banish him first for a 1000 years then for eternity as we read in the book of Revelation. Satan is attacking the population of the world as his end draws nearer so let us look at these three terrible events.

Famines

We have never witnessed the sorrow as we have seen in the last fifty years when millions have died in famines. Never have we heard of starvation like we have seen in Africa, both young and old have died. It has hit many other nations across the world but not on the scale that Africa has seen.

Pestilences

The world has also suffered in the last 50 years pestilences of all kinds. Nearly every part and organ of the human body can be attacked by cancer. Look at all the other pestilences such as V.D. infecting millions upon millions and this has spread to other nations. Its written Satan came into the world to kill, steal and destroy as we read in the book of Revelation.

Earthquakes

Earthquakes are happening over all the world as reported in the media. In the last 50 years over a thousand earthquakes have been recorded across many countries in the world when millions have been killed or injured. Remember our Lord has just said in verse 8 "all this is the beginning of sorrows".

PERSECUTION FOLLOWING THE REDUCING TIME SCALE TO THE LORD JESUS CHRISTS 2ND COMING

Verse 9 THEN THEY WILL DELIVER YOU UP TO TRIBULATION AND KILL YOU AND YOU WILL BE HATED BY ALL NATIONS.

In the last 25-30 years great persecution has arisen in many countries especially in Islamic, Hindu and atheistic countries and such as North Korea. As many as 250,000 Christians have been killed each year by extremists attacking churches and homes in remote villages where there is little protection. In Islamic countries they kill at will. This only begun in the last 25-30 years.

Jesus who created the world came into the earth to save people by his death on the cross and his resurrection. And those who believe and call upon his name will receive eternal life. By this he is showing Christ can proclaim the future from the beginning of time. And the book of Revelation shows Christ is able to proclaim end times in detail, so he is the Alpha and Omega, the first and the last, he is God.

Verse 12 THEN BECAUSE LAWLESSNESS WILL ABOUND THE LOVE OF MANY WILL WAX COLD.

Great Britain was once a Godly nation and God blessed us with one of the greatest empires in the world. In nearly every village there were approximately five or six churches and numerous ones in towns, but now, we have turned to ungodliness to become one of the worst nations in the world.

Thousands of Anglican Churches are standing empty all over the country. The Methodist Churches have sold thousands of churches that were empty and we are considering closing thousands more, besides many other denominations.

Sins and ungodliness have entered the Royal family and to every home in our land. We have lost our empire and our nations, like America, we are struggling for survival. God has warned us in the Bible of this evil of Satan in the world before the second coming of Jesus Christ. Our Lord has foretold us of the end of the world and the destruction Satan will accomplish before the end. So God has commanded us to repent to him and turn from our evil ways and he will save us, as every person has sinned all must repent to our Lord to be saved.

CHRISTIANS MUST FIGHT FOR THEIR FAITH TO THE END

Verse 13 HE THAT EDURETH TO THE END SHALL BE SAVED

Our Lord Jesus Christ was despised by his own people, rejected and endured crucifixion for us, so we are told to endure to the end to receive eternal life.

THE NEXT SIGN IN THE REDUCING TIME SCALE TO JESUS CHRIST'S SECOND COMING

Verse 14 AND THIS GOSPEL OF THE KINDOM WILL BE PREACHED IN ALL THE WORLD AS A WITNESS.

Therefore the end will not come until the Gospel is preached to all the world. This was our Lord's last instruction to his disciples in Mark chapter 16 verse 15.

Verse 15 "GO YE INTO THE WORLD AND PREACH THE GOSPEL"

Turning to Revelation chapter 14 verse 6 & 7.

I would like to speak of one of the major prophesies coming at the very end time and it is the same as spoken here in verses 6 & 7.

REVELATION CHAPTER 14 VERSES 6 & 7

Verse 6 THEN I SAW ANOTHER ANGEL FLYING IN MIDST OF HEAVEN HAVING THE EVERLASTING GOSPEL TO PREACH TO THOSE WHO DWELL ON THE EARTH – TO EVERY NATION, TRIBE, TONGUE AND PEOPLE

Verse 7 SAYING WITH A LOUD VOICE FEAR GOD AND GIVE HIM GLORY FOR THE HOUR OF HIS JUDGMENT HAS COME, AND WORSHIP HIM WHO MADE HEAVEN AND EARTH, AND THE SPRINGS OF WATER.

Billy Graham has just recently issued a statement that with modern day technology the gospel will have been preached throughout the world in the next Ten Years. I believe that Billy Graham was a mighty evangelist and if he is right only one main prophecy remains to be fulfilled before Jesus Christ comes, and this is found in the very next verse which is also found in Daniel chapter 9 the Abomination of Desolation spoken by Daniel the prophet and Matthew Chapter 24 verse 15.

ONE MAJOR PROPHESY TO FULFILL IN DANIEL CHAPTER 9 VERSE 27

DANIEL CHAPTER 9 VERSES 24 TO 27

Verse 27 THEN HE SHALL CONFIRM A COVENANT WITH MANY FOR ONE WEEK (IN ONE WEEK OF YEARS = 7 YEARS) BUT IN THE MIDDLE OF THE WEEK (3½ YEARS) HE SHALL BRING AN END TO THE SACRIFICE AND OFFERING. AND ON WING OF ABOMINATION SHALL BE ONE, WHO MAKES DESOLATION.

TO FULLY UNDERSTAND THE ABOMINATION OF DESOLATION

This is when Satan is cast out of Heaven to Earth to fulfil all his evil activity written in last 3½ years of the book of Revelation.

REVELATION CHAPTER 12 VERSES 7 TO 9

Verse 7 AND WAR BROKE OUT IN HEAVEN MICHAEL AND HIS ANGELS FOUGHT WITH THE DRAGON AND HIS ANGELS.

Verse 8 BUT THEY DID NOT PREVAIL, NOR WAS A PLACE FOUND FOR THEM ANY MORE IN HEAVEN.

Verse 9 SO THE GREAT DRAGON WAS CAST OUT THAT SERPENT OF OLD, CALLED THE DEVIL AND SATAN, WHO DECEIVES THE WHOLE WORLD HE WAS CAST TO THE EARTH AND HIS ANGELS WERE CAST OUT WITH HIM.

If you move to read chapter 13 verse 5 you find his allotted time he is allowed to reign (42 months 3½ years)

REVELATION CHAPTER 13 VERSE 5

Verse 5 AND HE WAS GIVEN A MOUTH SPEAKING GREAT THINGS AND BLASHEMIES AND HE WAS GIVEN AUTHORITY TO CONTINUE FOR FORTY TWO MONTHS (3½ YEARS) OR 1260 DAYS.

So what was written in Daniel chapter 9-27 corresponds with Matthew chapter 24-15 also corresponds with Revelation chapter 12 verse 7-9 and chapter 13 verse 5. This confirms without a shadow of doubt the truth of God's word.

SATAN TAKES HIS POSITION OF AUTHORITY IN JERUSALEM IN GODS TEMPLE

In 2 Thessalonians chapter 2 verse 3 and 4 it reads:

Verse 3 LET NO ONE DECEIVE YOU BY ANY MEANS FOR THAT DAY WILL NOT COME UNLESS THE FALLING AWAY COMES FIRST AND THE MAN OF SIN IS REVEALED, THE SON OF PERDITION.

Verse 4 WHO OPPOSES AND EXALTS HIMSELF ABOVE ALL THAT IS CALLED GOD OR THAT IS WORSHIPPED, SO THAT HE SITS AS GOD IN THE TEMPLE OF GOD, SHOWING HIMSELF THAT HE IS GOD.

Here Satan the Dragon in Revelation chapter 12 is cast into the earth and links up with the beast and the false prophet.

REVELATION CHAPTER 13

Verse 4 SO THEY WORSHIPPED THE DRAGON WHO GAVE AUTHORITY TO THE BEAST (MAN OF SIN) AND THEY WORSHIPPED THE BEAST; SAYING, "WHO IS LIKE THE BEAST? WHO IS ABLE TO MAKE WAR WITH HIM.

So Satan the dragon gave his authority to the beast the "Man of Sin" who had made a 7years Peace agreement in the Middle-East with 10 nations of the East and the world. Then at the end, Satan and the beast and false prophet and the ten nations armies of the East, will come over the River Euphrates. Then our Lord Jesus Christ will come and destroy them and take his waiting people home to heaven after the battle of Armageddon.

Let's read Revelation chapter 17 verses 12 to 14

Verse 12 THE TEN HORNS WHICH YOU SAW ARE TEN KINGS WHO HAVE RECEIVED NO KINGDOM AS YET, BUT THEY RECEIVED AUTHORITY FOR ONE HOUR AS KINGS WITH THE BEAST.

Verse 13 THESE ARE OF ONE MIND, AND WILL GIVE THEIR POWER AND AUTHORITY TO THE BEAST.

Verse 14 THESE WILL MAKE WAR WITH THE LAMB, AND THE LAMB WILL OVERCOME THEM, FOR HE IS LORD OF LORDS AND KING OF KINGS AND THOSE WITH HIM ARE CALLED CHOSEN AND FAITHFUL, AMEN.

So we are the chosen and faithful who are resurrected on that day (the day of our Lord coming).

SO THE REDUCING TIME SCALE IS DOWN TO THREE AND HALF YEARS

The very next verse proves that Christians must flee out of Judea to God's special place in the mountains.

MATTHEW CHAPTER 24 VERSE 16 TO 20

Verse 16 THEN LET THOSE IN JUDEA FLEE TO THE MOUNTAINS

This is a warning to all Christians to flee from Jerusalem and Judea in the last 3½ years when Satan links with the beast in this city in the midst of seven year peace agreement (A 7 years Covenant, then 3½ years).

Verse 17 LET HIM WHO IS ON THE HOUSE-TOP NOT GO DOWN TO TAKE ANYTHING OUT OF THE HOUSE.

They must leave quickly. All household goods must be left also leave your belongings.

Verse 18 AND LET HIM WHO IS IN THE FIELD NOT GO BACK TO GET HIS CLOTHES.

So leave all and obey Gods call to leave quickly.

Verse 19 BUT WOE TO THOSE WHO ARE PREGNANT AND TO THOSE WHO ARE NURSING BABIES IN THOSE DAYS.

Verse 20 AND PRAY THAT YOUR FLIGHT MAY NOT BE IN WINTER OR ON THE SABBATH.

Young mother or young mother to be, are under the Law of Moses, only allowed to travel a short distance on the Sabbath. So the bad weather may be against their flight also at this time.

There is also a corresponding account to this time found in Revelation chapter 12

Verse 14 BUT THE WOMAN WAS GIVEN TWO WINGS OF A GREAT EAGLE THAT SHE MIGHT FLY INTO THE WILDERNESS TO HER PLACE WHERE SHE IS NOURISHED FOR A TIME AND TIMES AND HALF A TIME FROM THE PRESENCE OF THE SERPENT (3½ YEARS – 42 MONTHS).

To a place of protection from the Lord.

MATTHEW 24 VERSES 21 TO 22

THE WORST DESTRUCTION EVER IS IN THE GREAT TRIBULATION

Verse 21 FOR THEN THERE WILL BE GREAT TRIBULATION SUCH AS HAS NOT BEEN SINCE THE BEGINNING OF THE WORLD UNTIL THIS TIME NOR EVER SHALL BE.

When you read of the destruction written in the 7 trumpets in Revelation chapter 8 to 11, it show that all the wars from the beginning of creation until this time cannot equal this devastation, where 2.2 billion people die, a third of the world's population.

The next verse shows the intervention of God

Verse 22 AND UNLESS THOSE DAYS ARE SHORTENED <u>NO FLESH</u> WOULD BE SAVED, BUT FOR <u>ELECT'S SAKE</u> THOSE DAYS WILL BE SHORTENED.

There must be hundreds of millions of Christians (The Elect) all across the world praying and crying out to God at this time, crying, "Come Lord Jesus, come and take thy waiting people home". So for the <u>Elect's sake "God stops it</u>". In the next few verses we see the coming of Christ for his Elect and the destruction of Satan's army; and all the ungodly people of the world who worship Satan and have his marks on their hand or head will die.

<u>REVELATION CHAPTER 13 VERSES 16 TO 18</u>

<u>MOST OF THE POPULATION OF THE WORLD RECEIVES SATAN'S MARK</u>

Verse 16 HE CAUSES ALL BOTH SMALL AND GREAT, RICH AND POOR, FREE AND SLAVE TO RECEIVE A MARK ON THEIR RIGHT HAND OR ON THE FOREHEAD.

Verse 17 AND THAT NO ONE MAY BUY OR SELL EXCEPT HE WHO HAS THE MARK OF THE BEAST OR THE NUMBER OF HIS NAME.

Verse 18 HERE IS WISDOM, LET HIM WHO HAS UNDERSTANDING CALCULATE THE NUMBER OF THE BEAST FOR IT IS THE NUMBER OF A MAN HIS NUMBER IS 666.

Satan is a liar and deceiver together with all his followers he sends his wicked lying prophets and teachers, into the churches as well as outside the churches, doing miraculous works such as fire from heaven as he did in Job's Day. He is the deceiver of the whole world.

CHRISTIANS WILL NOT BE DECEIVED BY EARTHLY SIGNS

<u>MATTHEW 24 VERSE 23 TO 26</u>

Verse 23 THEN IF ANYONE SAYS TO YOU LOOK HERE IS CHRIST! OR THERE! DO NOT BELIEVE IT.

Verse 24 FOR FALSE CHRISTS AND FALSE PROPHETS WILL RISE AND SHOW GREAT SIGNS AND WONDERS TO DECEIVE, IF POSSIBLE, EVEN THE ELECT.

Verse 25 SEE I HAVE TOLD YOU BEFORE HAND.

Verse 26 THEREFORE IF THEY SAY TO YOU, LOOK HE IS IN THE DESERT! DO NOT GO OUT, OR LOOK, HE IS IN THE INNER ROOM! DO NOT BELIEVE IT.

All these signs are earthly signs, this is what false prophets and teachers are saying at end times. But our Lord has warned us of them, so his Elect will not be taken by these earthly signs as God tells us in the very next verse of his heavenly signs revealed in the New Testament scriptures so many times.

CHRISTS HEAVENLY SIGNS FORETELLS OF HIS SECOND COMING

There are three heavenly signs in Matthew Chapter 24, verses 27 to 29 to the second coming of Christ.

Verse 27 FOR AS THE LIGHTENING COMES FROM THE EAST AND FLASHES TO THE WEST, SO ALSO WILL THE COMING OF SON OF MAN BE.

FIRST

Jesus Christ is coming in the clouds of heaven.

REVELATION CHAPTER 1 VERSE 7

Verse 7 BEHOLD HE IS COMING WITH CLOUDS AND EVERY EYE WILL SE HIM, EVEN THEY WHO PIERCED HIM, ALL THE TRIBES OF THE EARTH WILL MOURN BECAUSE OF HIM.

And all the ungodly will mourn with fear, for Christ comes in judgment on all those who worship Satan, and have accepted his mark or followed in his evil ways of sin. So Christ will have a heavenly visible entrance to the earth in glory. His entry will be to take all Christians home at the trumpet sound. We will meet him in the air for ever to be with our Lord.

Second

THE SECOND HEAVENLY SIGN

ANOTHER EVENT HAPPENS AT THAT TIME

Verse 28 FOR WHERE-EVER THE CARCASS IS THERE THE EAGLES WILL BE GATHERED TOGETHER.

To fully understand this event and sign we must read and understand that Satan gathered a vast army of 200 million on the border of the River Euphrates Revelation chapter 9-16-18. This army kills 2.2 billion men by Fire, brimstone and smoke in Revelation chapter 9 verses 14- to 16.

Remember our God is a righteous judge, whatsoever a man soweth so shall he reap. They killed a third of the population of the world in a nuclear war (fire, brimstone and smoke). So Christ at his coming destroys this army in a similar way as we read:

REVELATION CHAPTER 19 VERSES 17 TO 19

Verse 17 THEN I SAW AN ANGEL STANDING IN THE SUN AND WITH A LOUD VOICE HE CALLED TO ALL THE BIRDS THAT FLY IN MID-HEAVEN.

Verse 18 "COME, GATHER FOR THE GREAT SUPPER OF GOD."

Verse 19 TO EAT THE FLESH OF KINGS THE FLESH OF CAPTAIN, THE FLESH OF MIGHTY MEN AND THE FLESH OF HORSES AND THEIR RIDERS AND THE FLESH OF ALL MEN BOTH FREE AND SLAVE BOTH SMALL AND GREAT.

So God calls all the birds in mid-heaven to devour the carcases of this vast army after the battle of Armageddon as he spoke in Matthew chapter 24 verse 28.

THE THIRD AND FINAL HEAVENLY SIGN, SHOWING TWO EVENTS AT JESUS CHRIST SECOND COMING.

MATTHEW CHAPTER 24 VERSE 29 TO 31

Verse 29 IMMEDIATELY AFTER THE TRIBULATION OF THOSE DAYS SHALL THE SUN BE DARKENED, AND THE MOON SHALL NOT GIVE HER LIGHT AND THE STARS SHALL FALL FROM HEAVEN.

FIRST EVENT

Verse 30 AND THEN SHALL APPEAR THE SIGN OF THE SON OF MAN IN HEAVEN; AND THEN SHALL ALL THE TRIBES OF THE EARTH MOURN! AND THEY SHALL SEE THE SON OF MAN COMING IN THE CLOUDS OF HEAVEN WITH POWER AND GREAT GLORY.

SECOND EVENT

Verse 31 AND HE SHALL SEND HIS ANGELS WITH A GREAT SOUND OF A TRUMPET AND THEY SHALL GATHER TOGETHER HIS ELECT FROM THE FOUR WINDS, FROM ONE END OF HEAVEN TO THE OTHER.

Verse 30 shows “first event” when all the ungodly mourn at the coming of the Son of Man.

Verse 31 shows “second event” at the sound of the trumpet all the Elect are gathered by the Son of Man’s angels to heaven.

THE JUDGEMENT AND THE RESURRECTION BOTH COME ON THE DAY OF THE LORDS RETURN AS REVEALED IN REVELATION, AS YOU READ THE BOOK OF TWO EVENTS.

1. AT THE END OF THE 6TH SEAL
2. AT THE END OF THE 7TH TRUMPET AND AT THE END OF 2 REAPING IN CHAPTER 14

REVELATION CHAPTER 6 VERSE 12 TO 17

Verse 12 AND I BEHELD WHEN HE HAD OPENED THE SIXTH SEAL, AND LO THERE WAS A GREAT EARTHQUAKE; AND THE SUN BECAME BLACK AS SACKCLOTH OF HAIR AND THE MOON BECAME BLOOD.

Verse 13 AND THE STARS OF HEAVEN FELL TO EARTH AS A FIG TREE CASTETH HER UNTIMELY FIGS, WHEN SHE IS SHAKEN OF A MIGHTY WIND.

Verse 14 AND THE HEAVEN DEPARTED AS A SCROLL WHEN IT IS ROLLED TOGETHER AND EVERY MOUNTAIN AND ISLAND WERE MOVED OUT OF THEIR PLACES.

Verse 16 AND SAID TO THE MOUNTAIN AND ROCKS, FALL ON US, AND HIDE US FROM THE FACE OF HIM THAT SITTETH ON THE THRONE, AND FROM THE WRATH OF THE LAMB: (1ST EVENT – DEATH TO ALL SINNERS).

Verse 17 FOR THE GREAT DAY OF HIS WRATH HAS COME AND WHO SHALL BE ABLE TO STAND

THEN IN CHAPTER 7 VERSES 1 TO 8 HE TALKED OF 144,000 OF THE TWELVE TRIBES OF ISRAEL WHO ARE TO REIGN WITH CHRIST IN HIS MILLENNIAL REIGN (THE NEXT 1000 YEARS WITH CHRIST).

ALSO HE TALKS OF THE RESURRECTED SAINTS IN HEAVEN (THE 2ND EVENT - STILL IN THE SIXTH SEAL)

REVELATION CHAPTER 7 VERSES 9 TO 14

Verse 9 AFTER THIS I BEHELD AND LO A GREAT MULTITUDE WHICH NO MAN COULD NUMBER, OF ALL NATIONS, AND KINDREDS, AND PEOPLES, AND TONGUES STOOD BEFORE THE THRONE AND BEFORE THE LAMB CLOTHED WITH WHITE ROBES AND PALM BRANCHES IN THEIR HANDS.

Verse 10 AND CRIED WITH A LOUD VOICE SAYING SALVATION TO OUR GOD, WHICH SITTETH UPON THE THRONE AND UNTO THE LAMB.

Verse 11 AND ALL THE ANGELS STOOD ROUND ABOUT THE THRONE, AND ABOUT THE ELDERS AND THE FOUR BEASTS, AND FELL BEFORE THE THRONE ON THEIR FACES AND WORSHIP THE LAMB.

Verse 12 SAYING, AMEN; BLESSING AND GLORY AND WISDOM, AND THANKS GIVING, AND HONOUR, AND POWER, AND MIGHT BE TO OUR GOD FOR EVER AND EVER, AMEN.

Verse 13 AND ONE OF THE ELDERS ANSWERED SAYING "UNTO ME, WHAT ARE THESE WHICH ARE ARRAYED IN WHITE ROBES? AND WHENCE CAME THEY?"

Verse 14 AND I SAID UNTO HIM "SIR THOU KNOWEST", AND HE SAID TO ME "THESE ARE THEY WHO CAME OUT OF GREAT TRIBULATION AND HAVE WASHED THEIR ROBES, AND MADE THEM WHITE IN THE BLOOD OF THE LAMB".

In Matthew 24-15 it talked of the abomination of Desolation, spoken by Daniel the Prophet (in mist of 7 years agreement – 3½ years). Then in verse 21 – For theirs shall be great tribulation such as was not since the beginning of the world to this time, nor ever shall be. This happened just before he spoke of the two events, ie the judgement on the ungodly and the 1st Resurrection of the righteous as found in the Sixth Seal.

THE SECOND ACCOUNT TO THE 2 EVENTS IN THE 7TH TRUMPET

REVELATION CHAPTER 11 VERSES 15 TO 18

Verse 15 AND THE SEVENTH ANGEL SOUNDED AND THERE WERE GREAT VOICES IN HEAVEN, SAYING "THE KINGDOM OF THIS WORLD, ARE BECOME THE KINGDOMS OF OUR LORD AND OF CHRIST; AND HE SHALL REIGN FOR EVER AND EVER".

Verse 16 AND THE FOUR AND TWENTY ELDERS, WHICH SAT BEFORE GOD ON THEIR SEATS, FELL ON THEIR FACES AND WORSHIPPED GOD,

Verse 17 SAYING "WE GIVE THEE THANK O LORD GOD ALMIGHTY WHICH ART, AND WAS, AND ART TO COME, BECAUSE THOU HAST TAKEN TO THEE THY GREAT POWER AND HAST REIGNED".

Verse 18 AND THE NATIONS WERE ANGRY, AND THY WRATH IS COME, AND THE TIME OF THE DEAD (FIRST EVENT ON THE WICKED), THAT THEY SHOULD BE JUDGED, AND THAT THOU SHOULDEST GIVE REWARD UNTO THY SERVANTS TO PROPHETS (SECOND EVENT), AND TO THE SAINTS, AND THEM THAT FEAR THY NAME SMALL AND GREAT, AND SHOULDEST DESTROY THEM WHICH DESTROY THE EARTH (THEN BACK TO THE FIRST EVENT).

In verse 15 it speaks of our Lord reigning for ever and ever. Verse 18 shows 2 events happening at his coming. In event one, we see the ungodly nations throughout the world angry at his coming, because God's wrath has come, because they are destroying the world. Second event, speaks of the prophets and saints and all who fear his name, receiving their reward in the resurrection at that time - so the judgement and resurrection come together.

THE THIRD EXAMPLE IS FOUND IN THE TWO REAPINGS

The first reaping deals with the resurrection of the righteous.

REVELATION CHAPTER 14 VERSES 12 TO 16

Verse 12 HERE IS THE PATIENCE OF THE SAINTS; HERE ARE THOSE WHO KEEP THE COMMANDMENTS OF GOD AND THE FAITH OF JESUS.

Verse 13 THEN I HEARD A VOICE FROM HEAVEN SAYING TO ME "WRITE; BLESSED ARE THE DEAD WHO DIE IN THE LORD FROM NOW ON", "YES" SAYS THE SPIRIT, "THAT THEY MAY REST FROM THEIR LABOURS AND THEIR WORKS DO FOLLOW THEM."

Verse 14 THEN I LOOKED AND BEHOLD, A WHITE CLOUD, AND ON THE CLOUD SAT ONE LIKE THE SON OF MAN, HAVING ON HIS HEAD A GOLDEN CROWN, AND IN HIS HAND A SHARP SICKLE.

Verse 15 AND ANOTHER ANGEL CAME OUT OF THE TEMPLE, CRYING WITH A LOUD VOICE TO HIM WHO SAT ON THE CLOUD, "THRUST IN YOUR SICKLE AND REAP FOR THE TIME HAS COME FOR YOU TO REAP FOR THE HARVEST OF THE EARTH IS RIPE".

(Verse 12 shows)

This reaping shows they are the Saints of God who keep the commandments of God and of Jesus Christ who is coming to reap them to heaven at his coming.

THE SECOND REAPING IS THE JUDGEMENT ON THE UNGODLY

The second reaping is the wrath of God on the ungodly which follows on at the same time as the resurrection which, follows in the next few verses.

REVELATION CHAPTER 14 VERSES 17 TO 20

Verse 17 THEN ANOTHER ANGEL CAME OUT OF THE TEMPLE WHICH IS IN HEAVEN, HE ALSO HAVING A SHARP SICKLE.

Verse 18 THEN ANOTHER ANGEL CAME OUT FROM THE ALTAR, WHO HAD POWER OVER FIRE, AND HE CRIED WITH A LOUD CRY TO HIM WHO HAD THE SHARP SICKLE, SAYING, TRUST IN YOUR SHARP SICKLE AND GATHER THE CLUSTERS OF THE VINE OF THE EARTH FOR HER GRAPES ARE FULLY RIPE.

Verse19 SO THE ANGEL THRUST HIS SICKLE INTO THE EARTH AND GATHERED THE VINE OF THE EARTH, AND THREW IT INTO THE GREAT WINE – PRESS OF THE WRATH OF GOD.

Verse 20 AND THE WINEPRESS WAS TRAMPLED OUTSIDE THE CITY, AND BLOOD CAME OUTSIDE THE CITY, AND BLOOD CAME OUT OF THE WINEPRESS, UP TO THE HORSES BRIDLE, FOR ONE THOUSAND SIX HUNDRED FURLONGS.

A great army gathered around Jerusalem for the great battle with the Lord Jesus Christ at the place called ARMAGEDDON. This army had killed one third of the world's population (about 2.2 billion people).

REVELATION CHAPTER 9 VERSES 14 TO 15

Verse 14 SAYING TO THE SIXTH ANGEL WHO HAD THE TRUMPET, "RELEASE THE FOUR ANGELS WHO ARE BOUND AT THE GREAT RIVER EUPHRATES.

Verse 15 SO THE FOUR ANGELS, WHO HAD BEEN PREPARED FOR THE HOUR, DAY, MONTH AND YEAR, WERE RELEASED TO KILL A THIRD OF MANKIND.

So this army killed by fire, brimstone and smoke (nuclear war) and God being a just God, destroys them in the same way at Christ's coming.

As it describes here the winepress of the wrath of God and the blood from 200,000,000 people flowing like a river. God also sent birds to eat their carcases up.

So we find this prophesy the chapter written in Matthew Chapter 24 giving a perfectly identical teaching to Revelation the last 42 months – 3 ½ years or 1260 days.

So let us look up for the redemption of our body, soul and spirit will be united for ever at our Lords coming. Come Lord Jesus Christ, Amen.

THEORIES ON THE SECOND COMING.

Introduction

Many young Christians have been influenced, by the writings of expositors of the Bible, who came to their findings and joined one of three beliefs;

1. Pre-tribulation. 2. Mid-tribulation. 3. Post-tribulation.

The first, believe the rapture of the Church, comes before the tribulation begins.

Then second, that it comes halfway through the tribulation, believing that in the midst of the tribulation, they will be raptured out. Then the third, Post tribulation, the belief is that the rapture will come at the very end of all of the tribulation. The whole purpose of writing this book is to unite the Church into one belief, one body, one bride, looking for the one coming of Christ for his Church.

I began to study this book on Revelation, while I was a student at the Pentecostal Bible College, in the early 1970's at Mattersey, near Doncaster. Being a man in my forties, who had left school at the age of fourteen, with very little formal education, also my father and one of my older brothers, had died, before I reached the age of eleven.

My Mother was a born again Christian, and went out to work, as well as taking care of my other brother and sister, and myself. I went into the forces to do my national service in the Durham Light Infantry at the age of nineteen. Then I met my first wife, Helen, and we had two boys, Colin and Michael.

My first wife died at the age of only twenty-six years. (I myself was aged twenty-eight at that time) Just a week or so before she died, I was saved, and then baptised in the Spirit, who became my Comforter. A local minister visited my wife, in the hospital just before she died, and she too made her confession of Christ as Saviour.

Eighteen months later, I met a Salvation Army girl, called Ruth Brunskill, and we were married just six months later; Ruth raised my own two sons, as well as giving birth to our only daughter, Dawn and my third son, Mark. We now have Grandchildren and have been married over 49 years.

My early Christian life was spent reading through scripture continually. I also studied the Seven Foundation Truths by C.L.Parker (Hebrew ch.6 verses 1-2), which was a tremendous grounding in my early years. The author, was a lecturer at Oxford University, a Tutor, a fellow and Chaplain, who also taught at the Pentecostal Bible College, in the early 1930's.

Returning to my time in Bible College, one day I went into an Anglican church behind the college, talking to the Lord in prayer, about what little knowledge I had, especially regarding the book of Revelation. It was from this time, that he increased my hunger and thirst for His second coming, and especially for the book of Revelation.

The Bible College had just moved premises from Kenley, London, to Mattersey, in Yorkshire, and a new Principal had been appointed. He was self educated and a man of faith, whom God had blessed in Homiletics' and Hermeneutics'. For example, first, you find three or four headings, then splitting each heading into sub-headings, that you may then understand, the truth of the whole chapter. It was this method of studying, which helped me study the book of Revelation.

On leaving college after two years, God led me to the right job, as a caretaker at our local secondary school in Shildon. The working hours at the school attracted me, as I could start work at 6am until 10am, then 2pm until 6pm. This gave me four hours off during the day, to start my studies. At that time my wife Ruth, worked from 9am until 2pm, on her part-time job, so it all worked out very well. (Don't judge me wrongly, I love my wife, but I also love God and his word. So, what he had laid on my heart, was to fill my life for the next thirty years)

My early studies showed me, that the Book of Revelation, was divided into three headings:

PAST, PRESENT, and **FUTURE.**

Past

This covered only seven verses in the first chapter, and was referring to the vision of Christ which came to John on the isle of Patmos.

Present

This covered the next few chapters, the letters to the seven churches, which were scattered throughout Asia, but can be applied to any church in the world, for they all face the same problems today, as they did then.

Future

From chapter four, to chapter twenty two, John is called by the Glorified Lord who is equal in all knowledge to his Father, to write this last book of the Bible so that his Bride can follow all the events prior to his second coming. The last two chapters take us beyond his second coming to the New World.

So, I would like you to study this book of Revelation with me, verse by verse, from Chapter four, to the end.

REVELATION CHAPTER 4 VERSE 1

As I have said, I will try to divide the Chapters into a few major headings then sub headings, so as to understand the whole of the Chapters.

JOHN THE APOSTLE'S CALLING INTO HEAVEN

Verse 1 "AFTER THIS I LOOKED AND LO IN HEAVEN AN OPEN DOOR! AND THE FIRST VOICE, WHICH I HEARD SPEAKING TO ME LIKE A TRUMPET, SAID "COME UP HITHER, AND I WILL SHOW YOU WHAT MUST TAKE PLACE, AFTER THIS"

The first thing we notice, was that John's eyes saw an open door in Heaven, just like Stephen (Acts 7:55-56) when he was being stoned to death, he saw the Lord standing in heaven as he rose to greet him, on coming into heaven.

But here, John has been invited to witness for himself, many heavenly visions of future things, which he wrote down, and it became the last book of the Bible.

Immediately John's eyes were open and he saw an open door, then he heard a trumpet-like voice inviting him into heaven saying, "Come up here". Very few prophets in the Old Testament, had glimpses of God's throne, we know Isaiah did, in his book, Chapter 6 - as it is written, "I saw the Lord, High and lifted up, and his train filled the Temple". Ezekiel also wrote of seeing a vision of our Lord. So, John also was chosen, to record visions preceding the second coming of Christ, as the book proves time and time again. As many theologians have written their interpretations of the book of Revelation, hence the body of the Church is split into different divisions. This is the reason why we will study it verse by verse, so all may evaluate it for the truth.

REVELATION CHAPTER 4 VERSES 2-3

APOSTLES AND PROPHETS HAVE A SPECIAL ANOINTING OF THE SPIRIT TO REVEAL GOD'S TRUTH.

Verse 2 "AT ONCE I WAS IN THE SPIRIT, AND LOW, A THRONE STOOD IN HEAVEN, WITH ONE SEATED, ON THE THRONE."

It is the same Spirit of God, that came upon the prophets of both the Old and New Testaments, These men of God, spoke as they were moved by the Spirit of the Lord. They were moved supernaturally and spoke as the mouth pieces of the Lord. Many other terms were used for this anointing such as - 'The Spirit of the Lord', - 'The Hand of God', - 'The word of the Lord', when this happened, they became the Ambassadors, or the Mouth-piece of God, also, many moved in Supernatural Power, and were able to interfere with the laws of nature, i.e. RED SEA, - MANNA FROM HEAVEN, - JORDAN RIVER, one can go, on and on both in the Old and New Testament, revealing God's supernatural Powers.

JOHN REVEALS THE GLORY OF GOD'S THRONE

Verse 3 "AND HE WHO SAT THERE, APPEARED LIKE A JASPER AND CORNELIAN AND ROUND THE THRONE WAS A RAINBOW THAT LOOKED LIKE AN EMERALD."

This must be one of the few accounts of God's throne. If one thinks of the beauty of an earthly throne, how much more, God's throne will be in heaven, in all radiance, splendour, beauty, and glory for the God who created Heaven and the Earth. Look at the beauty of the fish of the sea, the multi colours of the different fish. Then look at the birds of the air, the splendour and beauty of the thousands of various kinds, scattered over the Globe. Then look at the earth, and the many colours, the green of the grass, blue skies, the multi-coloured flowers and the various fruits that we all eat, a mass of different colours.

REVELATION CHAPTER 4 VERSES 4-5

TWENTY FOUR ANGELIC ELDERS, SEATED ON THEIR THRONE BEFORE GOD

Verse 4 "ROUND THE THRONE WERE TWENTY FOUR THRONES AND SEATED ON THIS THRONE WERE TWENTY FOUR ELDERS."

Some Bible expositors have said these twenty four elders are a representation of the Raptured Church. One of the most popular Television Speakers on the second coming, quoted this as a truth. But, you must agree, John only heard the call "Come up here" I will show you what must be hereafter, and from his visions wrote the last book of the bible.

Other expositors base their theory from the King James Version, Chapter 5 verse 10 which would imply that they were speaking of themselves, not the Church. But, C. L. Parker who was a Chaplain, Fellow & tutor of the University College of Oxford and read only his Greek Bible, shows us that the Revised Standard Version corrects only a few mistakes from the King James Translation and this was one of them, speaking of the redeemed from the earth and they not, the 24 Elders, shall reign on the earth.

In my own personal studies over the last twenty five years and thousands of hours, I have noted other scriptures which confirm that these twenty four Elders were Angelic beings in 24 permanent seats before God, these worship him day and night since, they were created to this position before his throne, nearer than the rest of the Angels, who also worshipped him from being created.

(My first example which proves, in my view, is the numbers that come up in many chapters throughout Revelation such as seven seals, seven trumpets, seven vials,
Forty two months, one thousand two hundred and sixty days, these are not mere approximate, but the original numbers, so why take these twenty four Angelic beings, as anything less.)

My second evidence is their dress and crowns, they were clad in white garments with Golden crowns, in chapter seven verse nine, and the saints of God from earth at the coming of Christ, received Garments of white. Then in verse eleven it says all the Angels are gathered around

Gods Throne, and the twenty four Elders and the four living creatures as recorded in chapter four, before the rapture takes place.

Again in chapter fifteen verse six, and out of the temple came the seven angels with the seven plagues (vials) all robed in pure white bright linen. All the way through-out the book, Angels have white apparel.

These Elders have permanent seats and delegated authority as they cast their crowns before their Lord, recognizing He is Lord of Lords and King of Kings, the Almighty. Both Paul and Peter were looking for Crowns, Paul in 2nd Timothy, chapter four, verse eight said "Henceforth there is laid up for me a Crown of Righteousness which the Lord the righteous judge will award me on that day" (the day of Christ's coming)

Peter said in 1st Peter chapter five verse four, "when the chief Shepherd is manifested you will obtain the unfading crown of Glory." So Crowns are given when our Lord returns, when he appears the second time to take his waiting people home.

Going back to John's visions who was witnessing and writing things that will come upon the earth, prior to the day of the Lord, Our Lords second coming, which we shall prove again and again as we study this book.

REVELATION. CHAPTER, 4 VERSE 5-7

THESE ELDERS HAD GREATER REVELATION TO REVEAL TO JOHN

In Revelation chapter seven, verse thirteen, it states one of these Elders addressed John and told him of the millions and millions of saints that have just been translated from the earth after having passed through the great tribulation, like a soldier who has come out of the last war, (He has passed through it).

Again in Revelation chapter eleven verses fifteen to Nineteen, as the seventh Angel blows the seventh trumpet, these twenty four Elders began to sing a prophetic Song of Christ's kingdom, his everlasting kingdom has just arrived on earth. It is also a day of God's wrath for it says he will destroy those who are destroying the earth on that same day as the

Resurrection of the saint's and their reward in heaven. These Elders are actually singing a revelation of the rapture and judgement coming in one day. John had no idea of what he is witnessing until it is made known to him and he wrote it down for Christians on earth, so it is so important that we understand and be ready for His Coming.

THE SUPERNATURAL POWERS & MYSTERIES AROUND GOD'S THRONE

Verses 5 – 6 "FROM THEIR THRONE ISSUED FLASHES OF LIGHTNING AND VOICES AND PEALS OF THUNDER AND BEFORE THE THRONE BURN SEVEN TORCHES OF FIRE, WHICH ARE THE SEVEN SPIRITS OF GOD AND BEFORE THE THRONE THERE IS AS IT WERE A SEA OF GLASS LIKE CRYSTAL."

So powerful and mighty is God's word, that it illuminates all his throne by lightning, and thunder around his throne, in a supernatural way. Aaron the high priest in the tabernacle (Holy of Holy's) in the wilderness must have been terrified as he only went in once a year, but not without the blood of a spotless sacrifice for his sin, and the sins of the people. One day we shall enter heaven by the blood of the lamb Jesus Christ, this is the only way to heaven.

Also, in the tabernacles in the wilderness was a lamp stand, with seven lights that gave light to that part of the tent, so the tent in the wilderness was a replica given to Moses on the mountain of the original one in heaven.

THE MYSTERY OF THE CRYSTAL SEA BEFORE GOD'S THRONE

This heavenly sea of crystal glass is another mystery, if it is before God's throne it is of the utmost importance. If we think of the seas of the earth, they stretch for thousands of miles. We don't have very much written about this, I could make a suggestion but it may be mis-leading, and astray from the truth, so we will leave it a mystery.

THE FOUR LIVING CREATURES WHO MOVE WITH GOD

Verse 6 "AND ROUND THE THRONE ON EACH SIDE OF THE THRONE ARE THE FOUR LIVING CREATURES."

Verse 7 "FULL OF EYES, IN FRONT AND BEHIND"

Both in Ezekiel chapter one, and ten it speaks of these living creatures as Cherubim, in similar manner to these here, in the King James version it speaks of them as Beasts, in Revelation and living creatures in Ezekiel. I personally believe these are the same in Ezekiel as recorded here. The only difference is the four wings mentioned in Ezekiel and the six wings here. There was tremendous movement as they were flying and had to come to rest, in every other aspect they were equal. I cannot see God altering them in time. When we get to heaven we will see for ourselves these wonderful creatures before their God and their creator.

REVELATION CHAPTER 4 VERSES 8 - 11

ALL THESE CREATURES HAVE FOUR FACES

ONE - A FACE OF A LION

The first face was the face of a Lion, spoken of as King of the animal world; it's strong, very ferocious and has great strength when hunting. We remember Daniel was cast into the Lions den, and an Angel came and protected him so these living creatures may have control over all these faces that they portray.

SECOND - A FACE OF AN OX

Secondly there comes the face of an Ox, which gives us a different picture, as this was the largest of the animals sacrificed. So this may give the impression that they are wholly given to God and would gladly lay down their lives for their God.

THIRD - A FACE OF A MAN

Thirdly we have the face of a man, and as God gave them the power to master and rule on earth, these living creatures have power over mankind to exercise judgement, if they go beyond Gods laws, that their sins have reached up to heaven like certain cities and Kings, i.e. Sodom, Nineveh, King Herod, and others.

FOURTH - A FACE OF AN EAGLE

The fourth face is of an Eagle, which is the prize bird of the air. It has power to rise high above the storm clouds, and has such power and strength in its claws, wings and beak beyond any other of the birds. One may say that these are the Kings of the bird kingdom. So these living creatures watch over the areas of Gods Kingdom, this is my own suggestion. (?) Remember in Elijah days, birds were sent to feed him, also at the Second Coming of Christ, Millions of birds are gathered, to feed on the carcases of the dead at the battle of Armageddon.

REVELATION CHAPTER 4 VERSES 8 - 11

WORSHIP STARTS WITH THE LIVING CREATURES AND ESCALATES THROUGHOUT HEAVEN

Verse 8 "AND DAY AND NIGHT THEY NEVER CEASE TO SING, 'HOLY, HOLY, HOLY IS THE LORD GOD ALMIGHTY, WHO WAS AND IS, AND IS TO COME'."

Verse 9 " AND WHENEVER THE LIVING CREATURES GIVE GLORY AND HONOUR AND THANKS, TO HIM WHO IS SEATED ON THE THRONE, WHO LIVES FOR EVER AND EVER, THE TWENTY FOUR FALL DOWN, BEFORE HIM WHO IS SEATED ON THE THRONE, AND WORSHIP HIM WHO LIVES."

Verse 10 "FOR EVER AND EVER, THEY CAST THEIR CROWNS BEFORE THE THRONE, SINGING."

Verse 11 "WORTHY ART THOU OUR LORD AND GOD, TO RECEIVE GLORY AND HONOUR AND POWER FOR THOU DIDST CREATE ALL THINGS, AND BY THY WILL THEY EXISTED AND WERE CREATED."

The lyrics of the song holds tremendous truths and doctrines for they speak of God in the past tense, "who was" present tense" who is" and in the future tense " and is to come". He is the Almighty God who lives forever.

Also, let us remember that there are three persons in the God-head, Father, Son and Holy Spirit. It is very significant that these living creatures said "Holy, Holy, Holy, is the Lord God Almighty", as we have a Holy Father, The holy one of Israel, Jesus Christ, and the Holy Spirit, and all three persons are working together in our Redemption and Salvation.

Then, these twenty four Elders automatically and spontaneously began to worship the Lord. The worship escalates to all his angels in heaven, as the whole of heaven, is enveloped in Praise and Worship. The twenty four elders cast their crowns at the feet, of the Triune God, nothing is withheld, and they give all power and authority back to God, to whom they rightly belong.

So, let this be an example to all saints on earth, not to be taken up in this life in any authority both in the world or in the work of God, in any Ministry gifts, any spiritual gifts, or any status of any kind, for the main work of our Lord, is for us to have a Christ like nature, and to be holy, as he is holy.

So, let us not be caught up in this world as we hasten to the coming of the Lord, when our resurrection takes place, the redemption of our bodies, when mortality puts on immortality and corruption puts on in-corruption, when our last enemy, death is destroyed at the coming of Christ.

LET US LEAVE THIS CHAPTER FOUR, WITH THE MOTTO OF THE PENTECOSTAL BIBLE COLLEGE

"O Lord God Almighty, let me never lose the important truth, - to be in thy will, is better than success, and grant that I might ever love thee, more, than thy service."

REVELATION CHAPTER 5 VERSE 1

This chapter is a wonderful and remarkable chapter, for it reveals the equality of Father and Son in the Godhead and by the Spirit of the Lord, John is able to see and record many mysteries of Heaven.

We will endeavour to reveal some of the mysteries under the next few headings concerning Chapter Five.

1st Heading: THE MYSTERY BOOK HELD IN THE FATHER'S HAND

Verse 1 "AND I SAW IN THE RIGHT HAND OF HIM WHO WAS SEATED ON THE THRONE A SCROLL WRITTEN WITHIN AND ON THE BACK, SEALED WITH SEVEN SEALS."

This is God's book held safe in God the Father's hand. To be in the Father's hand is the safest place in the universe for no one is able to pluck anything from his hand. So, it is a safe and secure book.

As he loosens the seals we find it contains many mysteries, these seals have been a mystery to many expositors of this book. John was called up to heaven, to witness this prophetic book, and to write its content down for Christians, especially those living at the end times.

There are seven-seals which must be opened, and until we open each one, we cannot receive the full picture. When each seal is opened it is like a jig-saw puzzle which when joined together, gives a clearer view of the picture of the end times.

REVELATION CHAPTER 5 VERSES 2- 4

2nd Heading: A UNIVERSAL SEARCH, FOR A HOLY ONE, TO OPEN THE BOOK

Verse 2 "AND I SAW A STRONG ANGEL PROCLAIMING WITH A LOUD VOICE WHO IS WORTHY TO OPEN THE SCROLL AND BREAK ITS SEALS?"

Verse 3 "AND NO ONE IN HEAVEN OR ON EARTH OR UNDER THE EARTH WAS ABLE TO OPEN THE SCROLL OR TO LOOK INTO IT"

Angels are sent to reveal mysteries of the future, to Apostles, and Prophets, to pass on to the saints in his church. Then he asked John the question that he could not answer. Angels have very strong voices when proclaiming God's mysteries. This book in God's hand, must have the seals broken to open to us the mysteries of the future.

Only on a few occasions has God revealed the name of ministering angels such as Michael and Gabriel. It may be, people have a tendency to look to the minister, and not to God's word. Ministers pass away at death, but God's word abides forever, so let us look to the ministry of the word, and not to the minister.

Angels from God have supernatural ministry to search heaven and earth, and Hades, but no angel was found worthy. No earthly man was found in the early church of that time, also no patriarch from the Old Testament or saint or prophet, and no person in Hades, from the beginning of creation was able to open the book.

JOHN WEPT AT HOW SIN AFFECTED EVERY SPHERE OF GOD'S UNIVERSE.

Verse 4 "AND I WEPT, THAT NO ONE WAS FOUND WORTHY TO OPEN THE SCROLL OR TO LOOK INTO IT."

As one realises the depth of sin through-out God's creation, both in Heaven as well as on the earth and in Hades, and in our lives sin is the ruination of every person for it is written, all have sinned and come short of God's standard for Heaven.

If you think that all wars from the beginning of creation, have been caused by sin, every home that has split up, comes from sin, the deceiving wickedness and ungodliness has spread into every home, even heaven has been affected, so much, that not one Angel could open the book. This is what it would imply, so John wept bitterly.

REVELATION CHAPTER 5 VERSES 5 - 8

ONE OF THE TWENTY FOUR ELDERS REVEALS GOD'S SON IS ABLE TO OPEN THE BOOK.

Verse 5 THEN ONE OF THE ELDER'S SAID TO ME "WEEP NOT. LO, THE LION OF THE TRIBE OF JUDAH, THE ROOT OF DAVID, HAS CONQUERED, HE CAN OPEN THE SCROLL AND ITS SEVEN SEALS"

So after these three regions were searched for a successful person to open this book in God's hand, it took one of the twenty four elders before God's throne to reveal the hidden lineage of God's son Jesus Christ. He came out of the line of Judah, he was also the Lord who established David. He came from his offspring, "A Virgin shall conceive and bear forth a child and his name shall be called Emmanuel God is with us." Jesus was born to conquer sin, for he was tempted at all points as we are, yet was without sin, He conquered death, as he said, "I must go up to Jerusalem, be crucified and on the third day I shall rise again."

He conquered hell for all who believe in his name have Eternal Life. John was transformed from weeping, to strength, for he knew Christ as his Lord, his Saviour, and his Redeemer.

CHRIST IS ALSO, THE LAMB OF GOD WHO TAKES THE BOOK FROM HIS FATHER'S HAND

Verse 6 "BETWEEN THE THRONE AND THE FOUR LIVING CREATURES, AND AMONG THE ELDERS, I SAW A LAMB STANDIING AS THOUGH IT HAD BEEN SLAIN, WITH SEVEN HORNS AND SEVEN EYES WHICH ARE THE SEVEN SPIRITS OF GOD, SENT INTO ALL THE EARTH."

Verse 7 "AND HE WENT, AND TOOK THE SCROLL FROM THE RIGHT HAND OF HIM SEATED ON THE THRONE."

Always remember the four living creatures and the twenty four Elders around his throne, were in permanent positions. Then we see the Lamb of God in the centre of the throne, and we remember the words of John the Baptist, when he saw Jesus walking toward him, "Behold the Lamb of God that takes away the sin of the world" Then, linking the words of Isaiah "He was led as a Lamb to the slaughter" he goes on to say "He was wounded for our transgressions, he was bruised for our iniquities and by his stripes we are healed."

So, Christ died as our Redeemer and Saviour, and rose up victorious over death. Then, He ascended up to his Father to fulfil another scripture, "Sit thou at my right hand until I make your enemies your footstool" Here we see Christ as the Glorified Lord, equal with his Father again, to regain all power and knowledge and wisdom. He takes the prophetic book from his Fathers hand to open up the scripture, concerning the last three and a half years, before he comes again to take his waiting people home to Heaven. He said in the gospel of John "In my Fathers house are many mansions, I go to prepare a place for you, and if I go, I will return and receive you to myself that where I am there you may be also.

ALL HEAVEN EXPLODES IN WORSHIP TO THE FATHER AND SON'S ACHIEVEMENT

Verse 8 "AND WHEN HE HAD TAKEN THE SCROLL, THE FOUR LIVING CREATURES AND THE TWENTY FOUR ELDERS FELL DOWN BEFORE THE LAMB, EACH HOLDING A HARP AND WITH GOLDEN BOWLS FULL OF INCENSE, WHICH ARE THE PRAYERS OF THE SAINTS."

As soon as the Lamb of God took the book, they explode in worship both the elders and the living creatures, they fall before The Father and The Son, with musical instruments, and they play music before their Lord in worship.

They also act as Priests before God, interceding and having bowls of incense, a sweet smelling fragrance. They are interceding in prayer, for the Angels in heaven are very much involved with the saints on earth and are praying and working for their good. Many throughout the Bible were sent to bring insight, help, and assurance to his saints on the earth.

REVELATION CHAPTER 5 VERSES 9 - 10

THE WORDS OF THE SONG DECLARE CHRIST'S REDEMPTION WORK ON THE EARTH.

Verse 9 "AND THEY SANG A NEW SONG SAYING, WORTHY ART THOU TO TAKE THE SCROLL AND TO OPEN ITS SEALS, FOR THOU WAST SLAIN AND BY THY BLOOD DIDS'T RANSOM MEN FOR GOD FROM EVERY TRIBE AND TONGUE, AND PEOPLE AND NATIONS."

Verse 10 "AND HAST MADE THEM A KINGDOM AND PRIEST TO OUR GOD AND THEY SHALL REIGN ON THE EARTH."

First, we see Jesus Christ is the Holy one, and the only one worthy, to open up this prophetic last book of the Bible. As our Lord created the world in the beginning with his Father and the Holy Ghost, he also became our Redeemer, the redeemer of the world. For the life blood of the Son of God atones for the sins of the world. This is the reason he declares he will gather from across his globe, saints from every walk of life into the world to come. There is also a transforming power in the blood of Christ, not only to be saved but to transform us into Sons of God, not by words only, but walking daily against all the powers of evil which Satan brings against us, to stop us being transformed into Christ's image. Then we shall be priests in the world to come.

A Priest officiates to God, he is ordained to intercede, and be an example to others. Christ the great high priest was a perfect example in this life, he offered himself as a ransom for the world (Greater love hath no man than this, that Christ died for sinners) The whole plan of God can be seen in this verse in John 3 v.16 - For God so loved the world, that he gave his only begotten Son, that whosoever believes in him, shall not perish but have eternal life, So we are prepared for the Kingdom to come.

REVELATION CHAPTER 5 VERSES 11 - 14

THIS WORSHIP GATHERS MOMENTUM THROUGHOUT HEAVEN

Verse 11 "THEN I LOOKED, AND I HEARD AROUND THE THRONE AND THE LIVING CREATURES AND THE ELDERS, THE VOICES OF MANY ANGELS, NUMBERING MYRIADS OF MYRIADS, AND THOUSANDS OF THOUSANDS,"

Verse 12 "SAYING WITH A LOUD VOICE "WORTHY IS THE LAMB WHO WAS SLAIN, TO RECEIVE POWER AND WEALTH AND WISDOM, MIGHT AND HONOUR, GLORY AND BLESSING."

Verse 13 "AND I HEARD EVERY CREATURE IN HEAVEN AND ON EARTH, UNDER THE EARTH, AND IN THE SEA, AND ALL THEREIN SAYING, "TO HIM WHO SITS UPON THE THRONE, AND TO THE LAMB, BE BLESSING AND HONOUR AND GLORY AND MIGHT FOR EVER AND EVER"

Verse 14 "AND THE FOUR LIVING CREATURES SAID "AMEN" AND FELL DOWN, AND WORSHIPPED."

So worship spreads throughout the whole of heaven. This gathering was very special, to open this prophetic book of the end times on earth. This gathering is witnessed by all in heaven, for the first time, and at the same time as the Glorified Christ takes the book to reveal the contents (for the first time) to both the population of heaven and John the Apostle, so that he may write the last book of the Bible.

Millions assembled to worship what Christ had done on earth and on the cross. These Angels also knew of the Lamb of God's redemptive work which received recognition and worship from all his universe, heaven and earth, and under the earth and the sea. So these Angels in Heaven, worship the Lamb who gives all the opportunity to be redeemed from sin. He also reveals the dreadful attack of Satan, when he is cast out of heaven into the earth, and tries to do as much destruction as he possibly can, as we shall see in the last three and a half years.

In Revelation chapter 12, it tells us that Satan is cast out of heaven, then and then only, it says now has Salvation come into heaven, 2000 years after the cross of Christ. Satan is evicted from heaven, so, he is allowed 2000 years to repent of his evil deed of destroying, a third of the Angels in heaven, and billions on the earth, as it also declares (verse 12) "Woe unto the inhabitants of the earth, for the devil, has come down to you in great wrath."

So, the destruction which is written in the last book of the Bible, is what the wrath of Satan intends to do, when he is cast out of heaven. The Father, the Son, and Holy Spirit have planned the redemption work of the Son, Jesus Christ. and every believing citizen in Christ, rejoices in Him, when he opens the book, which reveals the final episode of Satan, and we will all say AMEN.

We must remember John was witnessing the future, the last three and a half years, when Satan will manifest himself in the earth, and it is recorded in so many ways, "The seven seals, and seven trumpets", then how he links with the beast and false prophet. In chapters 13 + 14, it reveals the two reapings on the earth one for heaven and one for hell. God has shown us many pictures of the end times for the benefit of his bride.

REVELATION CHAPTER 6 VERSES 1 – 8

JESUS CHRIST THE LAMB OF GOD HAS DIVINE RIGHT TO OPEN THE SEVEN SEALS.

Verse 1 "NOW I SAW, WHEN THE LAMB OPENED ONE OF THE SEVEN SEALS, AND I HEARD, ONE OF THE FOUR LIVING CREATURES SAY AS WITH A VOICE OF THUNDER, COME"

Our Lord gives ministries to his trusted Angels in heaven, and we will see many ministering Angels being used to reveal these mysteries hidden in this book. Even his disciples on earth walked three and a half years with their Lord before he made them Apostles and sent them to spread the Gospel around the world.

Yet there are fallen Angels like Lucifer, a Cherub, who ministered around Gods Throne, until he desired to be God, and became Satan, who corrupted the Angels in heaven, then attacked Adam and Eve, and the population of the world to transgress God's laws, and commandments, when they come to an age of understanding "Ye who are dead in trespasses and sins", its our trespasses that causes our spiritual death, not Adam's who sinned 6000 years ago. Coming back to this creature whom God entrusted, as a covering Cherub who surrounded his throne, and he is used to assist the Lord.

HOW SATAN RULES THE FIRST FOUR NATIONS WHO RIDE DIFFERENT COLOURED HORSES IN THE FIRST FOUR SEALS.

Verse 2 "AND I SAW AND BEHOLD A WHITE HORSE, AND ITS RIDER HAD A BOW: AND A CROWN WAS GIVEN TO HIM, AND HE WENT OUT CONQUERING AND TO CONQUER."

It is the rider that has been given a crown; he already had a weapon which he could use for either hunting or war. The crown was given him so he had authority, and as God allows people with authority to rule a nation, they are still accountable for their actions whether good or bad.

The next few words show he makes war with other nations, to rule more land and grow richer at the expense of many lives, both his own soldiers and the nation he attacks. He is very skilful and powerful in warfare, and goes from victory to victory and causes suffering to millions.

THE SECOND SEAL REVEALS A SECOND EVIL MAN

Verses 3-4 "WHEN HE OPENED THE SECOND SEAL I HEARD A SECOND LIVING CREATURE SAY "COME" (4) AND OUT CAME ANOTHER HORSE, BRIGHT RED, ITS RIDER WAS PERMITTED TO TAKE PEACE FROM THE EARTH, SO THAT MEN SHOULD SLAY ONE ANOTHER, AND HE WAS GIVEN A GREAT SWORD."

Again God uses the second living creature in the same way as the first creature by the word "Come" as though it was releasing what was held behind the seal.

The next horse was bright red, again its rider is an evil man. If these nations ask for this man, God may permit him to reign, but will still hold him accountable for his actions.

This rider, as we read, takes peace from the earth. Is this worldwide? As peace has been removed all over the earth, it has disappeared in people's hearts, in families, in homes and all areas of society. Some nations have had uprisings and wars, like many in Africa, causing suffering and taking peace from billions of people all over the world, so this rider is affecting the whole world.

THE MYSTERY BEHIND THIRD RIDER, ON THE THIRD HORSE.

Verses 5- 6 “WHEN HE OPENED THE THIRD SEAL, I HEARD THE THIRD LIVING CREATURE SAY, "COME" AND I SAW, AND BEHOLD A BLACK HORSE, AND THE RIDER HAD A BALANCE IN HIS HAND, (6) AND I HEARD WHAT SEEMED TO BE A VOICE IN THE MIDST OF THE FOUR LIVING CREATURES SAYING "A QUART OF WHEAT FOR A DENARIUS, AND THREE QUARTS OF BARLEY FOR A DENARIUS, BUT DO NOT HARM OIL AND WINE!”

Each living creature performs the same ministry; each said the same word "Come" to start the revelation behind each seal. The next horse to appear was black. Still the rider is un-named but he had balances in his hands, which showed he was in charge of food, as though there was a scarcity of food in some parts of the world. The prices for food rose, so that many poor would be unable to purchase enough to live on, in other words starvation would hit parts of the world, and no country has suffered starvation like many parts of Africa, this will happen more in the last three and a half years of Satan's reign on earth.

Even though inflation is running high in other parts of the world, I believe God is warning us to put our finances in order and budget for the days we are coming to, so let us be prepared as Christians should be, as the future looks very bleak as we read on.

HOW SATAN RULES THESE NATIONS AND RIDES HORSES IN THE FIRST FOUR SEALS.

Verses 7 – 8 "AND WHEN HE OPENED THE FOURTH SEAL I HEARD THE VOICE OF THE FOURTH LIVING CREATURE SAY "COME" (8) AND I SAW AND BEHOLD A PALE HORSE AND ITS RIDER'S NAME WAS DEATH, AND HADES FOLLOWED HIM; AND THEY WERE GIVEN POWER OVER A FOURTH OF THE EARTH, TO KILL WITH SWORD AND WITH FAMINE AND WITH PESTILENCE AND BY WILD BEASTS OF THE EARTH."

So each living creature was permitted to speak the same word of authority, in the first four seals, "COME". This is the first time the rider has been mentioned and his name reveals him as the devil, for death and Hades follow him. In Hebrews ch.2 v 14, it says that Christ through death, might destroy him who had the power of death, that it the devil. So the devil is the one who brings death and Hell in the earth. And here he is the rider, who rides and destroys in these four areas, the first four seals. Look at these riders who cause killing by sword, Famine, Pestilence and wild beast. It is Satan who reigns over all these beasts and nations, and is killing millions if not billions, in different nations throughout the world.

God only allows Satan, three and a half years before he imprisons him for a thousand years. In many nations there has been many beasts, who have caused uprisings within the nations, men can be called beasts as Satan gives to his own beast in Revelation ch.13 v1-2, the power to reign, but God still makes them accountable for their evil ways, just as he makes every beast accountable that has arisen from creation until now.

As our God is a just God, there will be a day in which he will judge the deeds of all men, and as he has declared in his word, the righteous are received into Heaven, and the wicked into Hell. And as we have all sinned, we all need a Saviour, his beloved son, Jesus Christ, the Saviour of the world.

As we move nearer and nearer to the end of our age we must all pass through this time of great tribulation, false doctrine has arisen saying this is Gods wrath being poured out? But this is not so, It is Satan's hour, when he is cast out of heaven and causes Great wrath on Earth Revelations Ch.12 verse 12 - but woe to you O earth and sea for the devil has come down in great wrath, Because he knows his time is short, only 42 months, God's wrath is poured out in the last day, on Satan's empire as we will prove as we read on, But God does pour vials out which are part of his wrath on the seat of Satan and all those who accept his mark, toward the latter end of the tribulation.

REVELATION CHAPTER 6 VERSES 9 - 10

THE SOULS OF SAINTS MARTYRED UNDER GOD'S ALTAR IN HEAVEN

Verse 9 "WHEN HE OPENED THE FIFTH SEAL, I SAW UNDER THE ALTAR IN HEAVEN, THOSE WHO HAD BEEN SLAIN FOR THE WORD OF GOD, AND FOR THE WITNESS THEY HAD BORNE."

Verse 10 "THEY CRIED OUT WITH A LOUD VOICE "O SOVEREIGN LORD, HOLY AND TRUE, HOW LONG BEFORE THOU WILT JUDGE AND AVENGE OUR BLOOD ON THOSE WHO DWELL UPON EARTH?"

Many Christians believe the rapture will come before the great tribulation, this theory has arisen in the past couple of hundred years, and many Christians have accepted this view without any private study, or diligently seeking, to see if this is true. This is one of the reasons I am taking this book verse by verse, so that you cannot be misled by taking verses out of the context and using this to support their view.

There are many incidents of Christian suffering, as a result of witnessing to God's word. Even at the present time, two thousand years after the crucifixion, it has been recorded that two hundred and fifty thousand Christians are dying throughout the world each year. When we are martyred for Christ, we are taken to a place under the altar in heaven, only our souls go to this place, our bodies are buried and the spirits return to God who gave them. (Ecclesiastes Ch.12, v. 7)

Here we see Paul speaking of the separation of these three parts, body, soul and spirit. Two parts are temporal, our bodies and spirit, only the third part is eternal. Our Lord said "Into thy hand I commend my spirit", and then it is written "thou shall not leave my soul in Hades". Then his body never saw corruption, even in the book of Job it is written "even though worms may eat my flesh yet in my flesh I shall see my God". So these souls were able to cry out to God for justice, as their blood was shed, for being children of the Lord.

REVELATION CHAPTER 6 VERSE 11

PREPARING SOULS FOR THE NEXT STAGE - OUR BODILY RESURRECTION.

Verse 11 "THEN THEY WERE EACH GIVEN A WHITE ROBE AND TOLD TO REST A LITTLE LONGER, UNTIL THE NUMBER OF THEIR FELLOW SERVANTS AND THEIR BRETHREN SHOUD BE COMPLETE, WHO WERE TO BE KILLED AS THEY THEMSELVES HAD BEEN."

These souls are under Gods altar, these souls don't have bodies, so the robes are for future use, as we see in the next chapter when the resurrection takes place, and they are standing dressed in white robes before God's throne, So we see a preparation comes first to prepare them for the very next stage, the resurrection of their bodies.

It also says they had to rest a little time longer, as many more must suffer and die like them. Until a certain number is complete. This shows the tribulation is still in progress and many more are being martyred for their faith in Christ.

I will put two views to the next line, which is the completion of the number martyred for Christ, as Satan and his angels have been cast out of heaven, forty two months prior to the end (Rev. 12 v 9-10, & Rev.13 v15) With all Satan's army of angels, cast out of heaven, there will be space for the sons of God to inhabit the Heavens.

The next view is that they may be only one hundred and forty four thousand (Rev. 14 v.1) who reign, with Christ in the world to come. Our Lord did say while on the earth, "they that suffer for me will also reign with me". So many more are to be martyred for Christ as he will create a new Heaven and a new Earth for millions to reign there in, so millions may be required to reign.

REVELATION CHAPTER 6 VERSES 12 - 14

THE SIXTH SEAL REVEALS A GEOGRAPHICAL CHANGE, BOTH ON EARTH AND IN THE HEAVENS.

Verse 12 – 14 "WHEN HE OPENED THE SIXTH SEAL, I LOOKED AND BEHOLD THERE WAS A GREAT EARTHQUAKE, AND THE SUN BECAME BLACK AS SACKCLOTH, THE FULL MOON BECAME LIKE BLOOD **(v 13)** AND THE STARS OF THE SKY FELL TO THE EARTH AS THE FIG TREE SHED IT'S WINTER FRUIT, WHEN SHAKEN BY A GALE **(v 14)** THE SKY VANISHED LIKE A SCROLL THAT IS ROLLED UP AND EVERY MOUNTAIN AND ISLAND WAS RE-MOVED FROM IT'S PLACE"

These signs recorded here, are also recorded in many places in the Bible, and are generally in the context of the coming of the Lord and the day of his judgement, in Matthew 24 v.29 it says immediately after the tribulation of those days, so we are in the tribulation, Christians are being persecuted all over the world. Then it goes on to say, the sun will be darkened and the moon will not give its light, and the stars will fall down from heaven, and the powers of heaven will be shaken.

In the Gospel of Luke, 21 v20, it also confirms the great tribulation when Jerusalem is surrounded by armies, that its desolation has come near. Then, v.25 gives this account; and there will be signs in the sun moon and stars, and upon the earth, nations in perplexity at the roaring of the sea, and men with foreboding of what is coming on the world, for the powers of the heavens will be shaken, then they will see the son of man coming in the clouds with power and great Glory. In Joel 2 v.10-11, Isaiah 2 v.18-19, Isaiah 13 v.10-11, also in Acts 2 v.19-20, all of these scriptures speak in the same way as the passage in Revelation, of Signs to the Coming day of the Lord.

REVELATION CHAPTER 6 VERSES 15 - 17

THE DAY OF CHRIST'S COMING IS THE DAY OF CHRIST'S WRATH

Verse 15-17 "THEN THE KINGS OF THE EARTH AND THE GREAT MEN AND GENERALS, AND THE RICH AND THE STRONG, AND EVERY ONE, SLAVE AND FREE, HID IN CAVES AND AMONG THE ROCKS OF THE MOUNTAIN'S, **(v16)** CALLING OUT TO THE MOUNTAINS AND ROCKS, "FALL ON US, AND HIDE US FROM THE FACE OF HIM WHO IS SEATED ON THE THRONE, AND FROM THE WRATH OF THE LAMB, **(v17)** FOR THE GREAT DAY OF THEIR WRATH HAS COME, AND WHO IS ABLE TO STAND BEFORE IT."

Fear will fill the heart of every person who is a sinner, for they have rejected the Lamb of God. They will try to hide behind rocks, and in caves, but no-one can hide from the judgment of the wrath of the Lamb, Our Lord, is seated on his throne, the King of Kings is ruling. The world of the ungodly will fear, and tremble for they have rejected the love of God, and spurned his atonement on the cross, for their sins. So that great day of his wrath comes on one single day. In one day, comes God's wrath and also on the same day, comes the resurrection of the sons of God, as we will read in the next chapter, a continuation of this chapter and the sixth seal. Our Lord spoke of the day, in Matthew 24 v 37. "as it was in the days of Noah, so will be the coming of the son of man, (v28) for in those days, before the flood, they were eating and drinking, marrying and giving in marriage, until the day when Noah entered the ark, and they did not know until the flood came and swept them all away" In the same day

Noah was saved the world perished. He also made reference to Lot in the Gospels, leaving Sodom, on the same day Lot was saved, all in Sodom perished, Emphasizing again the day of our Lord, is the day of our redemption, resurrection of our bodies and judgement for sinners, a just recompense for sin and ungodliness, they cried for rocks to fall on them, rather than come face to face before his throne, also the wrath of the Lamb, whom the world rejects.

REVELATION CHAPTER 7 VERSES 1 - 8

GODS ANGELS CALLED FOR SPECIAL MISSION, ON EARTH.

Verse 1 "AFTER THIS I SAW FOUR ANGELS STANDING AT THE FOUR CORNERS OF THE EARTH HOLDING BACK THE FOUR WINDS OF THE EARTH, THAT NO WIND MIGHT BLOW ON EARTH"

Verse 2 "THEN I SAW ANOTHER ANGEL, ASCEND FROM THE RISING OF THE SUN, WITH THE SEAL OF THE LIVING GOD, AND HE CALLED WITH A LOUD VOICE TO THE FOUR ANGELS WHO HAD BEEN GIVEN POWER TO HARM EARTH AND SEA,"

Verse 3 "SAYING, DO NOT HARM EARTH OR THE SEA OR THE TREES, TILL WE HAVE SEALED THE SERVANTS OF OUR GOD UPON THEIR FOREHEADS."

Our Lord uses many ministering angels in the Book of Revelation, but hardly any are mentioned by name. This would indicate, the message is more important, than the ministers, for they pass on at death, but God's word abides for-ever. Ministering Angels sent from God, usually have Supernatural powers given to them to fulfil their mission. These Angels were sent on a mission of destruction upon the earth, or a mission of judgement as they were able to hold back the North, South, East and West hurricane winds from all directions at the same time.

Then we see an Angel on a mission of mercy, to a hundred and forty four thousand of the tribes of Israel, to be saved and sealed. Four Angels, on a mission of Judgement and one Angel, on a mission of Mercy to a hundred and forty four thousand.

A SPECIAL REMNANT OF ISRAEL - SEALED, TO BE SAVED.

Verses 4 - 8 "AND I HEARD THE NUMBER OF THE SEALED, ONE HUNDRED AND FORTY FOUR THOUSAND, SEALED OUT OF THE TRIBES OF THE SONS OF ISRAEL."

	12,000	OUT OF THE TRIBE OF JUDAH
	12,000	OUT OF THE TRIBE OF REUBEN
	12,000	OUT OF THE TRIBE OF GAD
	12,000	OUT OF THE TRIBE OF ASHER
	12,000	OUT OF THE TRIBE OF NAPHTALI
	12,000	OUT OF THE TRIBE OF MANASSEH
	12,000	OUT OF THE TRIBE OF SIMEON
	12,000	OUT OF THE TRIBE OF LEVI
	12,000	OUT OF THE TRIBE OF ISSACHAR
	12,000	OUT OF THE TRIBE OF ZEBULUM
	12,000	OUT OF THE TRIBE OF JOSEPH
	12,000	OUT OF THE TRIBE OF BENJAMIN
	========	
TOTAL	= 144,000	OUT OF ALL THE TRIBES OF ISRAEL.
	========	

Notice two Tribes are missing, Ephraim and Dan. Our Lord, referred to a remnant, being saved out of Israel, in the book of Romans, 9 v 27. "THOUGH

THE NUMBER OF THE SONS OF ISRAEL BE AS THE SAND OF THE SEA, ONLY A REMNANT OF THEM WILL BE SAVED".

REVELATION CHAPTER 7 VERSE 9

THE RESURRECTION OF THOSE SAINTS AT THE END OF THE TRIBULATION

Verse 9 "AFTER THIS I LOOKED AND BEHOLD A GREAT MULTITUDE WHICH NO MAN COULD NUMBER, FROM EVERY NATION FROM EVERY TRIBE, AND TONGUE, PEOPLE STANDING BEFORE THE THRONE, AND BEFORE THE LAMB, CLOTHED IN WHITE ROBES, AND PALM BRANCHES IN THEIR HANDS."

Here is an innumerable company of Christians, translated to Heaven, who have passed through that great tribulation period, who have been raptured throughout the whole world, showing that persecution and tribulation is world wide, as the Anti-Christ is in control internationally and reigns universally. As the saints of our Lord are resurrected to Gods throne, and those under the altar in heaven are all presented with white robes to receive their bodies at the same time as the last trumpet sounds and the resurrection takes place, as all Christians are promised eternal life, who believe on Christ, are to be judged by Christ for our deeds done in the flesh, we inherit eternal life in heaven, or eternal life on earth, God will make a new heaven and a new earth, wherein dwells righteousness as it says, mortality must put on immortality, in John 5 v.28 it says, "Do not marvel at this; for the hour is coming when all that are in the grave will hear his voice (v.29) and come forth, those who have done good, to the resurrection of life, and those who have done evil, to the resurrection of judgement".

When we get to heaven we will know for certain if we are in heaven for ever, or on the earth, however where ever we find ourselves, we have an eternal future with our Lord, for we have Eternal Life. Also in John 14 v.1 it says, "In my Fathers house are many mansions, if it were not so, I would have told you. I go to prepare a place for you, and if I go to prepare a place, I will come again, and receive you to myself, that where I am, you may be also" Every Christian believer's hope is to be with Christ for ever.

REVELATION CHAPTER 7 VERSES 10 - 12

THESE RESURRECTED SAINTS CRY OUT IN PRAISE AND WORSHIP WITH THE HOSTS OF HEAVEN

Verse 10-12 (**v10**) CRYING OUT WITH A LOUD VOICE, "SALVATION BELONGS TO OUR GOD, WHO SITS UPON THE THRONE AND TO THE LAMB" (**v11**) AND ALL THE ANGELS STOOD, AND ROUND THE THRONE, AND ROUND THE ELDERS AND THE FOUR LIVING CREATURES, AND THEY FELL ON THEIR FACES BEFORE THE THRONE (**v12**) WORSHIPPING GOD SAYING "AMEN, BLESSING AND GLORY, AND WISDOM AND THANKSGIVING, AND HONOUR AND POWER AND MIGHT, BE TO OUR GOD FOREVER AND EVER, AMEN".

Everyone joins in worship to God and shout out like thunder, praising their Lord. The number praising is like the sand on the sea shore, and like the stars in the sky, for multitudes both those resurrected from earth and all those Angels who inhabit the Heavens, join in praise and worship, on this day, they praise God in unity and give worship and praise by every kind of word, describing God's character, by his Power, his might and his glory.

There is no other God so wonderful, so merciful and so glorious as our God who hath redeemed us from our sins and transformed us into sons of God, like his own beloved son, our Lord and Saviour, Jesus Christ and now resurrects us to his throne to live forever.

REVELATION CHAPTER 7 VERSES 13 - 14

AN ELDER GIVES UNDERSTANDING TO THE APOSTLE JOHN CONCERNING THE VISION.

Verse 13 "THEN ONE OF THE ELDERS ADDRESSED ME, SAYING "WHO ARE THESE CLOTHED IN WHITE ROBES, AND WHENCE HAVE THEY COME?"

Verse 14 "I SAID TO HIM, "SIR, YOU KNOW". AND HE SAID TO ME, "THESE ARE THEY, WHO HAVE COME OUT OF THE GREAT TRIBULATION, THEY HAVE WASHED THEIR ROBES AND MADE THEM WHITE IN THE BLOOD OF THE LAMB."

It took one of these twenty four elders to reveal what John saw in the sixth seal from the book, in our Lords hand. This proves that this angelic elder had greater understanding of the visions John was seeing and writing. An apostle of Christ had to be humble as a servant who answers the elder truthfully to his question "who are all these martyred saints in God's throne?" He truthfully answered "Sir, you know, I don't" Sons must be humble, if we remember in the first four seals we saw four Nations upon the earth with various powers of destruction and only one rider, whom we proved was the devil, and his influence or rule over all four powers.

Then in the fifth seal saints were murdered and martyred for Christ, this tribulation was still in progress as more martyrs were to be killed for their faith, their souls were under a special place in heaven, awaiting the next stage, to come after the tribulation, the resurrection of their bodies. "Coming out" simply means "passing through" like soldiers passing through the last war came out of it. In Matthew Ch.24 v.29 immediately after the tribulation, it describes Christ's coming, and his Angels gather his elect from one end of heaven to the other, they lay their lives on the altar of God, ready to suffer unto death, their faith in his blood cleanses their clothes, as though they had been washed white by his blood.

REVELATION CHAPTER 7 VERSES 15-16-17

CHRIST'S BLESSING TO THESE SAINT'S IN THE WORLD TO COME.

Verse 15 "THEREFORE ARE THEY BEFORE THE THRONE OF GOD, AND SERVE HIM DAY AND NIGHT WITHIN THE TEMPLE, AND HE WHO SITS UPON THE THRONE WILL SHELTER THEM WITH HIS PRESENCE."

Verse 16 "THEY SHALL HUNGER NO MORE, NEITHER THIRST ANY MORE, THE SUN SHALL NOT STRIKE THEM, NOR ANY SCORCHING HEAT."

Verse 17 "FOR THE LAMB IN THE MIDST OF THE THRONE WILL BE THEIR SHEPHERD AND HE WILL GUIDE THEM TO SPRINGS OF LIVING WATER, AND GOD WILL WIPE AWAY EVERY TEAR FROM THEIR EYES."

These have gained to be in our Lords throne for laying down their lives for an eternal reward, Our Lord will be their protection for their future, they may have hungered while on the earth but here, their provision will be sure, they will never thirst again for they are able to drink from the fountain of the water of life.

They may have been scorched on earth by the heat of the sun, while suffering at the hands of men, but they have the assurance of a perfect future for the Lord of Glory the Lamb of God, as their shepherd, who will provide their future and wipe away tears which they must have shed continually while on the earth, seeing friends and loved ones mutilated by those who have fallen under the evil power of Satan.

REVELATION CHAPTER 8 VERSES 1 - 5

Many Bible expositors believe the next four chapters have nothing to do with the end of the age, but as we examine these chapters they reveal Satan's evil power to bring destruction to the world. As we read and study our way through each chapter it reveals a picture of end times. All the seals, trumpets, thunders and vials fit together like a jig saw puzzle, that God wants every Christian to fully understand, each event concerning the great tribulation preceding the second coming of our Lord Jesus Christ. We will examine the next four chapters separately to fully understand the content of his message of the seven trumpets.

GODS MINISTERING ANGELS SANCTION THE SEVEN TRUMPETS REVEALING THE DESTRUCTION OF THE EARTH.

Verses 1-5 "WHEN THE LAMB OPENED THE SEVENTH SEAL, THERE WAS SILENCE IN HEAVEN FOR ABOUT HALF AN HOUR, (**v2**) THEN I SAW THE SEVEN ANGELS WHO STAND BEFORE GOD, AND TO THEM WERE GIVEN SEVEN TRUMPETS.(**v3**)THEN ANOTHER ANGEL HAVING A GOLDEN CENSER CAME AND STOOD AT THE ALTAR, HE WAS GIVEN MUCH INCENSE THAT HE SHOULD OFFER IT WITH THE PRAYERS OF THE SAINTS UPON THE GOLDEN ALTAR, WHICH WAS BEFORE THE THRONE. (**v4**) THE SMOKE OF THE INCENSE WITH THE PRAYERS OF THE SAINTS ASCEND BEFORE GOD, FROM THE ANGELS HAND (**v5**) THEN THE ANGELS TOOK THE CENSER FILLED IT WITH FIRE FROM THE ALTAR AND THREW IT TO THE EARTH, AND THERE WERE PEALS OF THUNDER, LOUD NOISES, FLASHES OF LIGHTNING AND AN EARTHQUAKE."

After much study on who this Priest coming out of the temple in Heaven could be, it is my personal belief that this is Melchizedek, Priest of the most high God (Hebrews 7 v1) who warned Abraham against taking any gift from Sodom before its destruction, and Christ became our Great High Priest with an eternal priesthood after the order of Melchizedek, who we see making the intercession at the heavenly altar, for the saints, before this destruction from Satan is allowed to come upon the earth. In times past, many Christians suffered unto death, and lived through times of great persecution and tribulation in many nations throughout the world; Death is no different in the Great Tribulation, only it is on a much larger scale. And as we read on, millions will pass into Eternity by wars, earthquakes, hurricanes Remember Jesus Christ is the Great High Priest in Heaven who has come into the temple with his own blood as the Lamb of God, who died for the sins of the world. So as King of Kings and Lord of Lords he is allowing everything to be fulfilled upon the earth as Gods prophets had predicted.

THE FIRST TRUMPET REVEALS SATAN'S DESTRUCTION ON LAND.

Verses 6-7 "NOW THE SEVEN ANGEL'S WHO HAD THE SEVEN TRUMPETS MADE READY TO BLOW THEM, THE FIRST ANGEL BLEW HIS TRUMPET AND THERE FOLLOWED HAIL AND FIRE, MIXED WITH BLOOD WHICH FELL ON THE EARTH AND A THIRD OF THE EARTH WAS BURNT UP AND A THIRD OF THE TREES WERE BURNT UP, AND ALL GREEN GRASS WAS BURNT UP."

When you study all of the seven trumpets, it is amazing how the world can endure these disasters that Satan is bringing upon the earth, Even our Lord said in Matthew 24 v21-23 speaking of the great tribulation, "if those days had not been shortened, no human being would be saved, but for the elect sake, those days will be shortened". So in these Angelic beings, blowing the trumpets, Christ is showing the Apostle John a vision two thousand years before the event, before our Lord's return.

At the sound of the first trumpet all hell seems to have broken loose upon the earth. It covers a wide area, i.e. a third of the earth. Man cannot imagine that a devastation of such magnitude could come upon us. But, we only have to look at the weapons of war invented by man, with one missile with nuclear warhead explosions which are able to destroy up to one hundred miles in each direction. Eastern countries like China and Russia have thousands of such weapons, also America, and many more countries. In Revelation Ch.12 v 12, when Satan is cast out of Heaven, it says "Rejoice then O Heaven and all who dwell therein, but woe to you earth and sea, for the Devil has come down to you in great wrath, because he knows that his time is short".

Revelations Ch.13.v 5, declares "He only has forty two months, three and half years or 1260 days" as Daniel, the prophet wrote in Ch.9 v 27. "Our Lord blesses the earth to multiply every plant and seed and fruit, till the earth is filled with the goodness of God", so in these latter days he is still feeding billions of people with daily food. (What a mighty God we serve.)

THE SECOND TRUMPET REVEALS SATAN'S ATTACK AT SEA.

Verses 8 – 9 "THE SECOND ANGEL BLEW HIS TRUMPET AND SOMETHING LIKE A GREAT MOUNTAIN BURNING WITH FIRE WAS THROWN INTO THE SEA. AND A THIRD OF THE SEA BECAME BLOOD A THIRD OF THE LIVING CREATURES IN THE SEA DIED, AND A THIRD OF THE SHIPS WERE DESTROYED."

We have just read of a great devastation which spread over one continent of the earth which exceeded tens of thousands of square miles. The second missile is fired into a sea, where there is an armada of ships. We must realize that John has to use his own terms to describe what he is witnessing to come in 2000 years, like a fiery mountain thrown into a sea. But look at the devastation caused in the sea, first it polluted the sea bed, a third of the fish in the sea died.

Let us just say, for instance this is in the Mediterranean. All the United Nation's ships would assemble if a war threatened and we lost a third of the western fleet. Look at the fear of such a disaster, with all the fishing vessels supplying millions of people, lost, and pleasure boats, then warships, then the fear and the roll-on effect it must cause much more misery to the nations of the world. Remember all this is happening because Satan has landed on earth and has only a short time to control it.

REVELATION CHAPTER 8 VERSES 10 - 11

THE THIRD TRUMPET DESCRIBES A WORLD WIDE BIOLOGICAL DISASTER

Verses 10-11 "THE THIRD ANGEL BLEW HIS TRUMPET AND A GREAT STAR FELL FROM HEAVEN, BLAZING LIKE A TORCH, AND IT

FELL ON A THIRD OF THE RIVERS AND ON THE FOUNTAINS OF WATER. (11) THE NAME OF THE STAR IS "WORMWOOD" A THIRD OF THE WATER BECAME WORMWOOD AND MANY DIED OF THE WATER BECAUSE IT WAS BITTER."

God only allows Satan certain powers of destruction, up to one third of the earth before he puts him away for a thousand years, Again as you analyse these two verses along with the two previous trumpets, one must come to the conclusion that it is a long range missile filled with a biological warhead, which is able to affect the water supply over a continent.

Look at the scientific and biological advancement made in laboratories, to use in warfare for killing the human population. In the past wars we find many code names given to these operations. It is man who decided what to call these terms of destruction, so the devil must be one who master-minded this operation and executed it.

Many more millions perish in this way, being poisoned by water, which God had given to be a fountain of life, as we cannot live without it, Satan's code name for this operation is "Wormwood".

REVELATION CHAPTER 8 VERSES 12 – 13

GOD ALLOWS SATAN TO INTERFERE WITH HIS HEAVENLY CONTELLATIONS IN THE FOURTH TRUMPET

Verse 12 "THE FOURTH ANGEL BLEW HIS TRUMPET, AND A THIRD OF THE SUN WAS STRUCK, AND A THIRD OF THE MOON AND A THIRD OF THE STARS, SO THAT A THIRD OF THEIR LIGHT WAS DARKENED, AND A THIRD OF THE DAY WAS KEPT FROM SHINING, AND LIKEWISE A THIRD OF THE NIGHT."

In the beginning these were created by God for the benefit of the world, Satan uses his evil powers to alter the lights of Heaven, for Satan is the god of darkness. He brings lies, deceit, to every man's heart, as God says, "All have sinned and come short of the glory of God, the standards fit for heaven. There is none righteous no not one". Here, he brings a third of the world into darkness. Whether he does this by nuclear warheads going off all over the world, we will have to wait and see, for what has been written will surely come to pass. In these four trumpets we have had;

1. Vegetation destroyed.
2. Contamination of the sea, and destruction of ships.
3. River and streams contaminated.
4. Interference with Sun, Moon and stars.

As Satan unleashes all the evil he can on all the earth.

SATAN LAST THREE TRUMPETS.

Verse 13 "THEN I LOOKED, AND I HEARD AN EAGLE CRYING WITH A LOUD VOICE, AS IT FLEW IN MID-HEAVEN, "WOE, WOE, WOE," TO THOSE WHO DWELL ON THE EARTH, AT THE BLASTS OF THE OTHER TRUMPETS WHICH THE THREE ANGELS ARE ABOUT TO BLOW."

This is one of the living creatures for in Revelation Ch.4 v.7, talking of these creatures it describes their four faces, one was a flying eagle, so these creatures seem to know what is behind each trumpet before they sound, we have just seen four woes described in the four trumpets, and still Satan's campaign of violence and destruction continues. All these scriptures in the book of Revelation, from Ch.4, interlink like a jigsaw, showing us the whole picture of the end times, for Revelation Ch.12, says when Satan is cast out of the heavens, "Woe unto the inhabitants of the earth, for the devil has come down to you in great wrath, because he knows that his time is short".

REVELATION CHAPTER 9 VERSES 1 - 2

All that is written, in the seven trumpets, happened in forty two months, (three and a half years, 1260 days.) as recorded in Revelation Ch.13 v.5. No wonder this is called the Great Tribulation period. When a Christian sees the truth and the revelation of end times scriptures, we can face it with an assurance that our Lord will descend from heaven at the last trumpet, when all the dead in Christ will arise from the grave and we that are left, and are alive, will meet him in the air, ever to be with our Lord. So let us see what the following three trumpets reveal to his body, the church.

THE ANGEL OF THE BOTTOMLESS PIT, AND HIS NATIONAL AND INTERNATIONAL ARMIES. (The first of 3 angels' revelation of the 3 woes.)

Verse 1 "THE FIFTH ANGEL BLEW HIS TRUMPET, AND I SAW A STAR, FALLEN FROM HEAVEN TO EARTH, AND HE WAS GIVEN THE KEYS OF THE SHAFT OF THE BOTTOMLESS PIT."

Verse 2 "HE OPENED THE SHAFT OF THE BOTTOMLESS PIT, AND FROM THE SHAFT ROSE SMOKE LIKE THE SMOKE OF A GREAT FURNACE AND THE SUN AND THE AIR WERE DARKENED WITH THE SMOKE FROM THE SHAFT."

This Angel of the bottomless pit, has many interchangeable names such as the beast of the bottomless pit, also other names such as Abaddon and Apollyon, the devil, and Satan, the great dragon, the deceiver of the world. Most of these, we will touch on, as we move through the book. In the book of Job, it tells how the stars sang together in the beginning, as angels of heaven. So Angels can be called stars. In Revelation chapter 12 v. 9, "The Dragon called Satan, the devil, is driven from heaven", here you have another picture of his activities in the earth, he has the keys to release his demonical power upon the earth. It is a true saying, "there is no smoke, without fire".

REVELATION CHAPTER 9 VERSES 3 - 6

THE SMOKE FROM THE FIRE, SCREENS SATANS ARMY.

Verse 3 "THEN FROM THE SMOKE CAME LOCUSTS ON THE EARTH, AND THEY WERE GIVEN POWER, LIKE THE POWER OF A SCORPION, ON EARTH..."

Verse 4 "THEY WERE TOLD NOT TO HARM THE GRASS OF THE EARTH OR ANY GREEN GROWTH OR ANY TREE, BUT ONLY MANKIND WHO HAVE NOT THE SEAL OF GOD ON THEIR FOREHEAD."

These locusts moved in tens of thousands, and in millions and in these words John is trying to give us understanding as to what he is seeing, i.e. an Army causing fire and smoke. These locusts, usually feed upon every green vegetation, but here they understand instruction and are disciplined to obey commands, and like Satan who was restricted when attacking Job, so this army is restricted at this time in their power over the Sons of God, i.e. they who have the seal of God on their foreheads.

THEY HAVE FRIGHTENING AND THREATENING POWER

Verse 5 "THEY WERE ALLOWED TO TORTURE THEM FOR FIVE MONTHS BUT NOT TO KILL THEM, AND THEIR TORTURE WAS LIKE THE TORTURE OF A SCORPION WHEN IT STINGS A MAN."

Verse 6 "AND IN THOSE DAYS MEN WILL SEEK DEATH AND WILL NOT FIND IT, THEY WILL LONG TO DIE, AND DEATH WILL FLY FROM THEM."

This army is also restricted with a limited time they are limited to five months, before their warfare is brought to an end. It doesn't say where in the world, but as everything recorded is literally connected with the Middle-east, we must assume this will be in that area. A scorpion has a sting that can kill, so each locust has the power to kill and also cause so many to fear their powers. They have the power to destroy mankind in that area.

REVELATION CHAPTER 9 VERSES 7 - 10

DESCRIBING THE ARMAMENT OF THIS NATIONAL ARMY.

Verse 7 "IN APPEARANCE THE LOCUSTS WERE LIKE HORSES, ARRAYED FOR BATTLE, ON THEIR HEADS WERE WHAT LOOKED LIKE CROWNS OF GOLD, THEIR FACES WERE LIKE HUMAN FACES."

Verse 8 "THEIR HAIR LIKE WOMENS HAIR, THEIR TEETH LIKE LIONS TEETH."

Verse 9 "THEY HAD SCALES LIKE IRON BREAST PLATES, AND THE NOISE OF THEIR WINGS WAS LIKE THE NOISE OF MANY CHARIOTS WITH HORSES RUSHING INTO BATTLE."

Verse 10 "THEY HAD TAILS LIKE SCORPION'S AND STINGS AND THEIR POWER FOR HURTING MEN FOR FIVE MONTHS LIES IN THEIR TAILS."

In verse seven it shows us a mobile unit or a fighting force, arrayed for battle. Each horse is described in the same way, a canopy like a crown over them. You must realise John had no idea of weapons of war, 2,000 years ago. He is actually in his own words describing a modern day fighting unit. Next he sees the face of a man operating this moving iron chariot, in verse 9 it talks of breastplates moving like a monster covered in armour plating, the noise of the engines frightening, like the sound of thousands of chariots rushing into battle, the noise both deafening and frightening.

May I bring in an illustration at this time? While doing my national service as an infantry man on manoeuvres in the middle of the night, our section embarked on the back of six tanks, they all seemed to start up at the same time, a deafening noise, which startled me, and was quite frightening, so imagine thousands of tanks rushing into battle at the same time the effect of the noise must have been terrifying, especially on the enemy.

With the latest weapons of war being modernized and upgraded every year, with long range guns, shells and rockets, we cannot even imagine what a future war will be like, I'm glad God only allowed this national army five months, and I can only think that the other army has had to surrender.

REVELATION CHAPTER 9 VERSES 11 - 16

THE NAMES OF THE KING WHO COMES AS THEIR COMMANDER

Verse 11 "THEY HAVE A KING OVER THEM, THE ANGEL OF THE BOTTOMLESS PIT; HIS NAME IN HEBREW IS ABADDON, IN GREEK HE IS CALLED APOLLYON."

Remember Satan is an angelic being, once was a cherub around God's throne. In Chapter 12 we see how he was defeated in heaven and how he fell to earth, he takes up another name, 'Angel of the bottomless Pit' when he enters the earth as king of this army in the middle east. This angel is also called the 'beast of the bottomless pit' for he killed Gods two servants in Jerusalem, again we see him in Rev.Ch.17 v.8. as the beast, that destroys Babylon the mother of harlots which we will come to in due time. So here, he is King of this national army.

THIS BEAST BECOMES KING OF AN INTERNATIONAL ARMY.

Verse 12 "THE FIRST WOE HAS PAST BEHOLD TWO WOES ARE STILL TO COME."

<u>Verse 13</u> "THEN THE SIXTH ANGEL BLEW HIS TRUMPET AND I HEARD A VOICE FROM THE FOUR HORNS OF THE GOLDEN ALTAR, BEFORE GOD."

<u>Verse 14</u> "SAYING TO THESIXTH ANGEL WHO HAD THE TRUMPET, "RELEASE THE FOUR ANGELS WHO ARE BOUND AT THE GREAT RIVER EUPHRATES."

<u>Verse 15</u> "SO THE FOUR ANGELS WERE RELEASED WHO HAD BEEN READY FOR THE HOUR, THE DAY, THE MONTH AND THE YEAR, TO KILL A THIRD OF MANKIND."

<u>Verse 16</u> "THE NUMBER OF THE TROOPS OF CAVALRY WAS TWICE TEN THOUSAND TIMES TEN THOUSAND, I HEARD THEIR NUMBER."

If you think of the first four trumpets and the devastation caused in each trumpet, and here we see his fifth trumpet as one woe, and two more woes to come. Then he describes the sixth trumpet, the second woe, and the greatest army ever assembled on the earth. The number of this army is two hundred million, who have just destroyed a third of the population of the world. In the last war approximately 50 million died in the world, so this devastation which in number is about 2.1 billion, is absolutely beyond our comprehension.

I personally believe only nuclear long range missiles can achieve this, and as both great nations America in the West and the Russian nation in the East, have hundreds of thousands of long range missiles which are capable of destroying this number. Then we see this army assembling on the borders of the Middle East and Israel as this last battle takes place around Jerusalem at Armageddon (Revelation.ch.16.v.12-16). We can see all this chapter and book portray the <u>end</u> times, and all interlink, and fit like a jig-saw puzzle, showing a perfect picture along with other scriptures, both in the Old and New Testaments.

Look at the time system, in Daniel (Revelation Ch.12-13) three and a half years. We see Satan, the Dragon, the Beast and false prophet as seen in Revelation Ch.13, after Satan is cast out of heaven, he links up with these other two accomplices. After this they are put away at the end of this age seen in scripture Revelation chapter 14 and Revelation chapter 20. Satan has 42 months, three and a half years, and these two armies took 5 months (Revelation Ch. 9 verse 10) and 13 months (Revelation Ch. 9 verse 14-15), which is 18 months of his allotted time.

So Christians are able to prepare themselves for Christ's coming, they should be prepared at any time to die for our saviour as he did for us, and how many are dying all through this tribulation period. He showed in Rev.ch.6 v.9 the souls slain for the testimony and many more are to die. The coming of Christ is just round the corner at this time, which is when our resurrection takes place. Let us look up with a full assurance that our redemption is just round the corner, the redemption of our bodies.

REVELATION CHAPTER 9 VERSES 17 - 19

HIS INTERNATIONAL ARMY IS DESCRIBED IN A SIMILAR WAY TO HIS NATIONAL ARMY.

Verse 17 "THIS WAS HOW I SAW THE HORSES IN MY VISION, THE RIDER WORE BREASTPLATES THE COLOUR OF FIRE AND OF SULPUR AND THE HEADS OF THE HORSES WERE LIKE LION HEADS, AND FIRE AND SULPHUR ISSUED FROM THEIR MOUTH."

Verse 18 "AND BY THESE PLAGUES A THIRD OF MANKIND WAS KILLED, BY THIS FIRE AND SMOKE AND SULPHUR, ISSUED FROM THEIR MOUTH."

Verse 19 "FOR THE POWER OF THE HORSES IS IN THEIR MOUTH, AND IN THEIR TAIL, AND THEIR TAILS ARE LIKE SERPENTS WITH HEADS, AND BY MEANS OF THEM, THEY WOUND."

In the last war, Russia was building one thousand tanks per month, so at the end of the war, they had tens of thousands of tanks. If you think of all the long range missiles fitted in the last few years, to the thousands of tanks built in the last 50 years, what an army could arise, as Satan gathers 10 nations from the east. (Daniel Ch.7 v. 7-20). This army of 200,000,000 destroys up to one third of the world population and vegetation before the battle of Armageddon.

Satan has come down from heaven knowing he has a short time, 42 months and he intends to destroy as many human souls on the earth as he possibly can, and leads this vast army to their doom along with himself. He knows very well the power God allowed him, and God has left this account for every Christian to read. So study and be prepared for the end is at hand. Many Christians are babies in the faith and never grow to maturity. God wants us to be ready like the five wise virgins, not the foolish (Matthew Ch.25) who have no idea of the time of his coming, He wants faithful and wise servants, (Matthew Ch.24 v. 44-46) who the Lord will find, doing and teaching the truth when he comes. They will be well rewarded in Eternity.

REVELATION CHAPTER 9 VERSES 20 - 21

GOD COMMANDS ALL MEN TO REPENT, AND BE DELIVERED FROM IDOL WORSHIP.

Verse 20 "THE REST OF MANKIND WHO WERE NOT KILLED BY THESE PLAGUES, DID NOT REPENT OF THE WORKS OF THEIR HANDS, NOR GAVE UP WORSHIPPING DEMONS AND IDOLS OF GOLD AND SILVER AND BRONZE AND STONE AND WOOD, WHICH CANNOT EITHER SEE OR HEAR OR WALK;"

Verse 21 "NOR DID THEY REPENT OF THEIR MURDERS OR THEIR SORCERIES, OR THEIR IMMORALITY OR THEIR THEFTS"

Repentance is one of the seven foundation truths in Hebrews ch.6 v 2, and God commands all men to repent, and turn away from their sin. The God of this world, Satan has exalted riches as an idol for man to seek after, with all of their hearts. That which man gives himself to fully, becomes his idol, and he lists many idols above and most people in the world are under the influence of Satan's temptation.

Christ said " I am the resurrection and the life" and our faith in him brings us an eternal future, no one can repent unless repentance is preached, so we must have a preacher, also we must have ears to hear, but even the hearing doesn't guarantee faith to salvation, but responding to Christ's call to repent. Here men still cling to the evil of the world, the love of money and immorality.

CHAPTER 10 & CHAPTER 11, STILL COME UNDER THE SIX TRUMPETS.

So it actually runs at the same time as the period we are describing, the three and a half years, or forty two months, Satan's manifesting himself, as we shall see and understand as we read on.

REVELATION CHAPTER 10 VERSES 1 - 4

IDENTIFYING AN ANGELIC HEAVENLY MINISTRY.

Verse 1 "THEN I SAW ANOTHER MIGHTY ANGEL COMING DOWN FROM HEAVEN, WRAPPED IN A CLOUD, WITH A RAINBOW OVER HIS HEAD, AND HIS FACE WAS LIKE THE SUN, AND HIS LEGS LIKE PILLARS OF FIRE."

When we talk of a mighty Angel, they are mighty because of their faithfulness and love for God. They are entrusted with great ministries. The glory that surrounds them is supernatural, since he is enveloped in a rainbow. Also like Moses when he came from Mount Sinai, his face shone with Gods glory, so this angel's face shone as he came from God. Always remember that Angels are sent to minister to the heirs of salvation with messages from God. All ministries are for the building up of the body of Christ on earth, Ephesians Ch.4 v.11-13 This Angel also came to John to give instruction, and direction in what he must do, and to pass on this message to the body of Christ.

JOHN WAS INSTRUCTED WHAT TO DO WITH THE BOOK AND THE 7 THUNDERS.

Verse 2 "HE HAD A LITTLE SCROLL OPEN IN THIS HAND, AND HE SET HIS RIGHT FOOT ON THE SEA AND HIS LEFT FOOT ON THE LAND. (**v3**) AND HE CALLED OUT WITH A LOUD VOICE LIKE A LION ROARING, WHEN HE CALLED OUT, THE SEVEN THUNDERS SOUNDED. (**v4**) AND WHEN THE SEVEN THUNDERS SOUNDED, I WAS ABOUT TO WRITE, BUT I HEARD A VOICE FROM HEAVEN SAYING "SEAL UP WHAT THE SEVEN THUNDERS HAVE SAID, AND DO NOT WRITE IT DOWN"."

This angel sent from God had supernatural power he was able to stand on sea and land together; he was also given a loud voice for proclaiming God's instruction, and brought with him seven thunders. These thunders were instruction of what is to come? as the seven seals and the seven trumpets revealed what is going to happen in the last times as well, Why, Why, Why, was John stopped from writing? In each of these events we have seen different pictures of the same period of time, so are the seven thunders another picture of that time? After the seventh trumpet sounded it declares "Christ's coming" Revelation.Ch.11 v.15-18. Then we read in Chapters 12,13,&14, of how Satan is cast out of heaven, his activities on earth for 42 months, and the two reaping at the end of times, just as the 7 seals and 7 trumpets recorded.

REVELATION CHAPTER 10 VERSES 5 - 7

THE ANGEL'S REVELATION ON WORSHIP AND THE SOUND OF THE LAST TRUMPET.

Verse 5 "THE ANGEL WHOM I SAW STANDING ON SEA AND LAND LIFTED HIS RIGHT HAND TO HEAVEN,"

Verse 6 "AND SWORE BY HIM WHO LIVES FOR EVER AND EVER, WHO CREATED HEAVEN AND WHAT IS IN IT, THE EARTH, AND WHAT IS IN IT, AND THE SEA AND WHAT IS IN IT, THAT THERE SHOULD BE NO MORE DELAY."

Verse 7 "BUT THAT IN THE DAYS OF THE TRUMPET CALL TO BE SOUNDED BY THE SEVETH ANGEL, THE MYSTERY OF GOD, AS HE ANNOUNCED TO HIS SERVANTS THE PROPHETS, SHOULD BE FULFILLED."

Look at this angel's prayers and worship. Even Christians say the same (more or less), in worship. We lift up our hands to God, we also acknowledge him, that he is our eternal Father, who created heaven and earth, and the sea and all that is therein.

We read his word as born again Christians, born of Christ the living word, and worship him as this Angel does, yet he knows that the seventh trumpet brings to an end, all that is written, all the mysteries written by the prophets of old, and the apostles of the New Testament.

So the last of the seals and the last trumpet reveals the last of what is written before the resurrection of the Saints takes place, and a judgement for all evil people, those who were destroying God's creation.

REVELATION CHAPTER 10 VERSES 8 - 11

JOHN RECEIVES INSTRUCTION ABOUT THE BOOK IN THE ANGEL'S HAND

Verse 8 “THEN THE VOICE I HEARD FROM HEAVEN SPOKE TO ME AGAIN, SAYING "GO TAKE THE SCROLL WHICH IS IN THE HAND OF THE ANGEL, WHO IS STANDING ON THE SEA AND THE LAND.”

Verse 9 “SO I WENT TO THE ANGEL AND TOLD HIM TO GIVE ME THE LITTLE SCROLL AND HE SAID TO ME "TAKE IT AND EAT IT, IT WILL BE BITTER TO YOUR STOMACH, BUT SWEET AS HONEY IN YOUR MOUTH.”

Verse 10 “AND I TOOK THE LITTLE SCROLL FROM THE HAND OF THE ANGEL, AND ATE IT. IT WAS SWEET AS HONEY IN MY MOUTH, BUT WHEN I HAD EATEN IT MY STOMACH WAS MADE BITTER.”

Verse 11 “AND I WAS TOLD YOU MUST AGAIN PROPHESY ABOUT MANY PEOPLE AND NATIONS AND TONGUES AND KINGS.”

This book and the contents must be sanctioned from heaven, the book has more revelation just like the seven seals, and the seven trumpets do. It holds the content of the seven thunders? We do know it was sweet as honey as he devoured the content in his mouth, all fresh and nice as he ate it, but after digesting God's Revelations of the book, after he had time to penetrate it into his soul, it became bitter, the revelation was bitter once he had understanding of the last days.

The word of this book, and the revelation from it, is for the world’s population, a world message, a world illumination as it is prophetic.

Remember we are still in the sixth trumpet, and still more is to be revealed in chapter eleven, it is important to understand what is revealed in chapter eleven before the final trumpet sounds.

REVELATION CHAPTER 11 VERSES 1 - 6

GOD'S INSTRUCTION TO JOHN REGARDING THE TEMPLE AT JERUSALEM. (In end times)

Verse 1 "THEN I WAS GIVEN A MEASURING ROD LIKE A STAFF, AND I WAS TOLD "RISE AND MEASURE THE TEMPLE OF GOD AND THE ALTAR, AND THOSE WHO WORSHIP THERE. **(v2)** BUT DO NOT MEASURE THE COURT OUTSIDE THE TEMPLE; LEAVE THAT OUT, FOR IT IS GIVEN OVER TO THE NATIONS AND THEY WILL TRAMPLE OVER THE HOLY CITY FOR FORTY TWO MONTHS. (Three and a half years is 1260 days.)

We are still in the sixth trumpet; things are still to happen before the seventh trumpet. He is talking of end times a temple in Jerusalem was to be measured only on the inside, where the Altar and Priests are, and worship is performed. But outside this area, the outer court, many people from across the nations are still occupying and assembling. At end times a time system is set up in this holy city, to occupy it for 42 months, the same time as Satan is cast out of heaven in the next 3 chapters, but we also see him in the next few verses with another of his names.

GOD'S TWO WITNESSES REVEAL THAT GOD IS STILL IN CHARGE OF THE END TIMES

Verse 3 "AND I WILL GRANT MY TWO WITNESSES POWER TO PROPHESY FOR ONE THOUSAND TWO HUNDRED AND SIXTY DAYS,

CLOTHED IN SACKCLOTH. **(v4)** THESE ARE THE TWO OLIVE TREES AND THE TWO LAMPSTANDS WHICH STAND BEFORE THE LORD OF THE EARTH, **(v5)** AND IF ANYONE WOULD HARM THEM FIRE POURS FROM THEIR MOUTH, AND CONSUMES THEIR FOES; IF ANYONE WOULD HARM THEM, THEN HE IS DOOMED TO BE KILLED. **(v6)** THEY HAVE THE POWER TO SHUT THE SKY THAT NO RAIN MAY FALL DURING THE DAYS OF THEIR PROPHESYING AND THEY HAVE POWER OVER THE WATERS TO TURN THEM TO BLOOD AND TO SMITE THE EARTH WITH EVERY PLAGUE AS OFTEN AS THEY DESIRE."

Here we have God's two witnesses arising within Jerusalem, to prophesy. They are prophets sent from God, and the time of their ministry is to last as long as Satan's activity on the earth.

These two are remarkable prophets, since God refers to them in the same way as the two prophets he raised up in the Old Testament, who stood as lamp stands and as olive trees, when he brought Israel out of the captivity after seventy years in Babylon. Their names were Zerubbabel and Joshua. They encouraged the people of God, when they were building up the walls of Jerusalem, to fulfil the first prophesy of the three major prophesies spoken, in the book of Daniel, Chapter 9 verses 24-27 of those years, (to be a week of years, (70 x 7) = Four hundred and ninety years.) = 490

1st THE RETURN AND THE CONSTRUCTION OF JERUSALEM

Prophesy 1. Seven weeks, of Seven years, is 7 x 7 years = 49

2nd THE FULFILMENT OF ALL THE MESSIAH PREDICTIONS.

Prophesy 2. Sixty two weeks, of Seven years, is 62 x 7 years = 434

3rd PEACE AGREEMENT BROKEN IN ISRAEL AND THE NATIONS.

Prophesy 3. Comes after indefinite period in midst of the 7 year peace agreement = 7

Then the tribulation comes in the midst of 7 year,

1260 days or three and a half years. = 490

It is at this time that Satan is cast out of heaven, for the last three and a half years. Satan's kingdom on earth starts shortly after these two prophetic witnesses arrive in Jerusalem to start their ministry and these two witnesses stand with great power in a similar way as Moses did against Pharaoh in Egypt, he also brought many plagues against the whole nation of Egypt, and every Egyptian suffered tremendously before Pharaoh was destroyed.

God allows these two witnesses to plague all of Satan's army and every person who received Satan's mark etc is to suffer, so God is not giving Satan an easy time, just as Satan is not giving the Christians an easy time. He is killing many of them for their faith all over the world.

REVELATION CHAPTER 11 VERSES 7 - 9

GOD IDENTIFIES THEIR ASSASSIN AND ALLOWS THEM TO DIE.

Verse 7 "AND WHEN THEY HAD FINISHED THEIR TESTIMONY, THE BEAST THAT ASCENDED FROM THE BOTTOMLESS PIT WILL MAKE WAR UPON THEM AND CONQUER THEM AND KILL THEM."

Verse 8 "AND THEIR DEAD BODIES WILL LIE IN THE STREETS OF THE GREAT CITY WHICH IS ALLEGORICALLY CALLED SODOM AND EGYPT WHERE THEIR LORD WAS CRUCIFIED.**V.9** FOR THREE AND A HALF DAYS, MEN FROM TRIBES AND TONGUES AND NATIONS GAZE AT THEIR DEAD BODIES AND REFUSE TO LET THEM BE PLACED IN A TOMB."

God will not allow any servants who are ministering his word to die, until he is ready; Some prophets live a short time, i.e. "John the Baptist" when his ministry ended, God allowed him to die, as many other prophets as in Matthew 23 v 34-35, "Therefore I send you prophets and wise men and scribes some of whom you will kill and crucify and some you will scourge in your synagogues and persecute from town to town". Other prophets he allowed to live until old age, as they had a ministry like John the apostle, who was witnessing and who wrote this final book.

In Chapter 9, we were told of an Angelic Being, coming down from Heaven who was called the Angel of the bottomless pit, who had great authority in the City of Jerusalem, the very place he desired to take up residence, as it is written of him in 2nd.Thessalonians.Chapter 2.verse 4, "who opposes, and exalts himself, against every so called god or object of worship, so that he takes his seat in the temple of God, proclaiming himself to be God".

It goes on to say that Christ Jesus will come and slay him with the breath of his mouth and the brightness of his coming. Not only is Satan evil but all mankind who sin from an early age of understanding, follows in Satan's footsteps as he influences the world, he hates God and his two servants he and the world do not want their bodies to be buried.

REVELATION. CHAPTER, 11 VERSE 10 - 12

GOD'S RIGHTEOUS SERVANTS WERE RESURRECTED BEFORE THEIR EYES.

Verse 10 "AND THOSE WHO DWELL ON EARTH WILL REJOICE OVER THEM AND MAKE MERRY AND EXCHANGE PRESENTS BECAUSE THESE TWO PROPHETS HAD BEEN A TORMENT TO THOSE WHO DWELL ON THE EARTH."

Verse 11 "BUT AFTER THE THREE AND A HALF DAYS A BREATH OF LIFE FROM GOD ENTERED THEM, AND THEY STOOD UP ON THEIR FEET, AND GREAT FEAR FELL ON THOSE WHO SAW THEM."

Verse 12 "THEN THEY HEARD A GREAT LOUD VOICE FROM HEAVEN SAYING TO THEM "COME UP HERE" AND IN THE SIGHT OF THEIR FOES THEY WENT UP TO HEAVEN IN A CLOUD."

The world hates Christians, for even now two hundred and fifty thousand each year are being murdered by extremists, and evil men. This number will increase as the end draws near. The world's population in general rejoices at the death of these two servants of God who were afflicting the world with many plagues.

Then God reverses the situation in a moment of time. Have you realized how Christians would feel as they hear and see how God used these two witnesses for three and a half years against the beast, what an uplift it must have been to Christians scattered all over the world as many were laying down their lives for the Lord Jesus.

Then there came another great move of God, their resurrection to glory, in the sight of the world. (This was probably viewed on T.V. by satellite) they witnessed them ascending into heaven, before their eyes. This is a pre-view of our resurrection which awaits us, for it is just round the corner, when the resurrection comes at the seventh trumpet, this will also speak volumes to the world, that their judgement is also just around the corner.

REVELATION CHAPTER 11 VERSES 13 - 15

GOD'S JUDGEMENT ON JERUSALEM PROCEEDING CHRIST'S COMING.

Verse 13 "AND AT THAT HOUR THERE WAS A GREAT EARTHQUAKE AND A TENTH OF THE CITY FELL; SEVEN THOUSAND PEOPLE WERE KILLED IN THE EARTHQUAKE, AND THE REST WERE TERRIFIED AND GAVE GLORY TO THE GOD OF HEAVEN."

So the beast in Jerusalem is taking a battering from our Lord, by the power of the resurrection of his two servants, also a judgement upon Jerusalem, by an earthquake and many had a change of heart in Jerusalem to give the God of heaven glory. This happens before the coming of our Lord Jesus Christ.

GOD'S FINAL TRUMPET, THE LAST TRUMPET AND THE FINAL WOE.

Verses 14 - 15 "THE SECOND WOE HAS PAST BEHOLD THE THIRD WOE IS SOON TO COME. (**v15**) THEN THE SEVENTH ANGEL, BLEW HIS TRUMPET, AND THERE WERE LOUD VOICES IN HEAVEN SAYING "THE KINGDOM OF THE WORLD HAS BECOME THE KINGDOM OF OUR LORD AND OF HIS CHRIST AND HE SHALL REIGN FOR EVER AND EVER".

It has been two thousand years since Christ got the victory over Satan, and it has taken two thousand years before he is cast out of heaven, Revelation Chapter 12 v 9, after a battle with Michael, leader of God's army. All these things begin to happen in the last three and a half years so it has taken 2,000 years before victory comes to heaven, Salvation then comes to heaven, and then the Kingdom of God and of Christ comes in power.

When the last trumpet sounds, Christ puts the last nail in to Satan's coffin, and then begins his reign on earth, for a thousand years, and after that, to reign for ever and ever.

REVELATION CHAPTER 11 VERSES 16 - 19

WORSHIP BREAKS OUT IN HEAVEN AS CHRIST BEGINS HIS REIGN ON EARTH

Verse 16 "AND THE TWENTY FOUR ELDERS, WHO SIT ON THEIR THRONES BEFORE GOD, FELL ON THEIR FACES AND WORSHIPPED GOD,"

Verse 17 "SAYING "WE GIVE THANKS TO THEE LORD GOD ALMIGHTY WHO ART AND WAS, THAT THOU HAST TAKEN THY GREAT POWER AND BEGUN TO REIGN."

Verse 18 "THE NATIONS RAGED, BUT THY WRATH CAME, AND THE TIME OF THE DEAD TO BE JUDGED, FOR REWARDING THY SERVANTS, THE PROPHETS AND SAINTS, AND THOSE WHO FEAR THY NAME, BOTH SMALL AND GREAT, AND FOR DESTROYING THE DESTROYERS OF THE EARTH."

When these elders began to worship, it was as if they were prophesying. They began with falling before their Almighty God. God works in the fullness of time. From the beginning of creation until Christ came for our redemption from sin, was four thousand years, and from then to now, is two thousand years. Our God is longsuffering, willing that none should perish. He gives time for transgressors to repent. But everything is in his hands. He is the first and last, and there is no other God before him. Now is the time for God to fully take control of his creation.

The nations will rage angrily at his coming. Remember that the day of Christ's coming has two events happening on the same day, In Matthew chapter 24 verse.30 ' then all the tribes of the earth will mourn, and they will see the Son of Man coming on the clouds of heaven, with power and great glory, and he will send out his angels with a loud trumpet call, at the same time he will gather his elect from the four winds, at the trumpet sound'. It is then he says the resurrected Christians will be judged, the resurrection takes place and everyone will give an account of their deeds done in the body, another event on that day - he will destroy those who are destroying the earth, The Beast who we have seen in all the 7 trumpets, and the destruction he has caused in the earth in his 42 month reign.

In Revelation Chapter 6, v 16, it talks of the world hiding from Christ on his throne. There is the glory of his throne and a judging of the people who mourn, "that thy wrath has come", all this happens on 'the same Day', as is illuminated in Matthew chapter 24, verses 38 - 39 when it says "on the same day Noah entered into the Ark, he was saved, and the world perished". God also took Lot from Sodom and one family was saved, and the others perished all in the same day. Below is verse 19 which may look a bit mysterious, but as you take an overall view of the whole book, as I said before, it fits, just like a jig saw puzzle, as revealed in Revelation Chapter 15, verse 18; THE TEMPLE WAS CLOSED UNTIL THE 7 PLAGUES

WERE POURED OUT. HERE ITS REOPENED AFTER THE 7TH TRUMPET SO THEY ALL INTERLINK.

So the seven vials must be completed at the same time as the seventh Trumpet is completed. The temple was closed before the seven vials were poured out at the battle of Armageddon, when all Satan's armies are all linking together to one coming, when the resurrection takes place and the judgement on the Devils peoples filling the earth.

GOD RE-OPENS HIS HEAVENLY TEMPLE, WHICH HE HAD CLOSED.

Verse 19 "THEN GOD'S TEMPLE IN HEAVEN WAS RE-OPENED, AND THE ARK OF HIS COVENANT WAS SEEN IN THE TEMPLE; AND THERE WERE FLASHES OF LIGHTING, LOUD NOISES, AND PEALS OF THUNDER, AN EARTHQUAKE AND HEAVY HAIL."

The temple in heaven will be opened at the end of the seventh seal, the seventh trumpet, (seven thunders?) and at the end of the seventh vial, as everything is completed in God's word, all mysteries, all prophesies, all scripture is fulfilled, and Christ will reign.

REVELATION CHAPTER 12 VERSES 1 - 2

THE MYSTERY OF THE WOMAN WITH CHILD.

Verse 1 "AND A GREAT PORTENT APPEARED IN HEAVEN, A WOMAN CLOTHED WITH THE SUN, WITH THE MOON UNDER HER FEET, AND ON HER HEAD A CROWN OF TWELVE STARS,"

Verse 2 "SHE WAS WITH CHILD, AND SHE CRIED OUT IN HER PANGS OF BIRTH, IN ANGUISH OF HER DELIVERY."

To fully understand these two verses in this chapter we must realize that we have seen the activity of Satan in the earth in the 7 seals then the 7 trumpets. This chapter carries on in the same vein, Satan as the dragon on earth attacking the three areas of the churches.

To fully understand the mystery of the woman, she represents the Christian church in Jerusalem and Israel and the church is under great pain and distress as she is travailing at the birth of a child who represents many Jewish believers who are translated to heaven as the first fruits of those martyred for Christ in and around Jerusalem, and are called to rule with Christ in the world to come.

This will all happen when Satan takes up his position in the temple in Jerusalem, recorded in 2nd.Thessalonions chapter 2 verses 3-4. The Mother Church in Israel is clearly seen as the light of the world with the sun and moon around her and the twelve apostles of the Lamb in the crown she is wearing.

In the next two chapters we see Satan's plan of attack on the Universal Church, also in Chapter 14 verses 1-5 it speaks of 144,000 who are redeemed and special before God's throne in Heaven, and are only ones who can sing a special song, these first fruits for God and the Lamb and no lie was found in their mouths for they were spotless. This is my own opinion, so we will have to wait until we come to heaven to see if it is true.

REVELATION CHAPTER 12 VERSES 3 - 5

THE MYSTERY OF THE DRAGON WHO IS SATAN

Verse 3 "AND ANOTHER PORTENT APPEARED IN THE HEAVEN; BEHOLD A GREAT RED DRAGON, WITH SEVEN HEADS, TEN HORNS, AND SEVEN DIADEMS UPON HIS HEADS."

Verse 4 "HIS TAIL SWEPT DOWN A THIRD OF THE STARS OF HEAVEN AND CAST THEM TO THE EARTH, AND THE DRAGON STOOD BEFORE THE WOMAN WHO WAS ABOUT TO BEAR A CHILD,

THAT HE MIGHT DEVOUR HER CHILD WHEN SHE BROUGHT IT FORTH."

Verse 5 "SHE BROUGHT FORTH A MALE CHILD, ONE WHO IS TO RULE ALL NATIONS WITH A ROD OF IRON. BUT HER CHILD WAS CAUGHT UP TO GOD AND HIS THRONE,"

Here we have an account of Satan's evil powers in deceiving a third of the population in heaven, it would imply by his seven heads, ten horns and seven diadems, that he ruled a great empire in heaven, this also shows Angels are an easy target to be deceived to transgress God's commandments and law's as man had done on earth, one cannot imagine a perfect cherub falling to become as any evil man, like i.e. Hitler, Stalin and hundreds more, and that he used his wisdom and knowledge to deceive a third of the Angels in heaven.

Do you realize God still allowed him 2,000 years in heaven after his beloved son was crucified for the sins of the world, and rose from the grave to justify men and give them a hope in a resurrection to heaven, to all who believe, but here the dragon is cast out of heaven and takes up his throne in Jerusalem.

It is at this time that a certain number are martyred for their faith to rule in the world to come, then the Mother Church was told to flee for refuge into the wilderness in the very next verse after he fails in an attempt to deceive the Mother Church he attacks the Universal Christian Church worldwide, in Verse 17.

REVELATION CHAPTER 12 VERSE 6

GOD PREPARED A HAVEN IN THE WILDERNESS

Verse 6 "AND THE WOMAN FLED INTO THE WILDERNESS WHERE SHE HAS A PLACE PREPARED BY GOD, IN WHICH TO BE NOURISHED FOR ONE THOUSAND TWO HUNDRED AND SIXTY DAYS."

The Gospels relate how Christ's second coming, is at the end of the time of the abomination of desolation, when Satan sits in the temple of God, showing himself as God. It is at this time he warns Christians in Judea and Jerusalem to flee into the wilderness or the mountains where God has prepared a place for them.

When Satan is cast out of heaven, as told in the next few verses, he takes up residence in the temple at Jerusalem; 2 Thessalonians Chapter.2 verses 3 - 4, this shows to every Christian worldwide, that God is still ruling, and at the end of forty two months the resurrection will take place. So every Christian has this great hope of his coming.

Remember, God's two servants who gave Satan a harassing time before they are resurrected, to bear witness to all who lived at Jerusalem. This three and a half year time system all corresponds with Daniel, chapter nine, when Gabriel was sent by God to reveal the last three and a half years, of a seven year peace agreement, when the abomination of desolation is set up.

Here God is preparing all Christians both in Jerusalem and across the world, some to move out of Jerusalem, and others to be prepared for any persecution as the resurrection is just around the corner, since Satan has completed all that he planned to do against the world, which our Lord so perfectly revealed in the book of Revelation and by the prophets.

REVELATION CHAPTER 12 VERSES 7 - 9

THE DEFEAT OF THE DRAGON AND HIS ANGELIC ARMY IN HEAVEN.

Verse 7 "NOW WAR AROSE IN HEAVEN, MICHAEL AND HIS ANGELS FIGHT AGAINST THE DRAGON; AND THE DRAGON AND HIS ANGELS FOUGHT,"

Verse 8 "BUT THEY WERE DEFEATED AND THERE WAS NO LONGER ANY PLACE FOR THEM IN HEAVEN,"

Verse 9 "AND THE GREAT DRAGON WAS THROWN DOWN, THAT ANCIENT SERPENT WHO IS CALLED THE DEVIL, AND SATAN, THE DECEIVER OF THE WORLD HE WAS THROWN DOWN TO THE EARTH AND HIS ANGELS WITH HIM."

How long this war lasted in heaven, only God knows, it has been two thousand years, since Christ died and rose again, and has ascended to his Father's side, and one may ask the question, why has God tolerated the Devil for another two thousand years? After Christ's resurrection the only scripture that springs to mind is that God is long suffering forbearing, and willing that none should perish.

We know Satan has many names as we have seen in this book, here we see him as the dragon linked with other names such as Ancient Serpent, deceiving the whole world, The ancient Serpent who tempted Adam and Eve to sin, and going on to deceive every person in the world, but finally God had enough of him, and drives him out of heaven to earth.

In the New testament we see Jesus referring to him as Beelzebub, the prince of Devils. In Rev. Chapter 9, we see other names connected with Satan, the Angel of the bottomless pit, the Beast, Abaddon, Apollyon, the Dragon, false Prophet and the Beast of the bottomless pit. The beast and the false prophet are simply in league with the dragon who killed two servants of God in Jerusalem as in Revelation Chapter 11 v 7. We remember Satan sitting in the Temple of God reigning in Jerusalem so when he is cast out, he takes up residence in God's holy City.

REVELATION CHAPTER 12 VERSE 10

THEN JOY BREAKS OUT IN HEAVEN WHEN SATAN AND HIS ARMY ARE CAST OUT.

Verse 10 "AND I HEARD A LOUD VOICE IN HEAVEN, SAYING "NOW THE SALVATION AND THE POWER AND THE KINGDOM OF

OUR GOD AND THE AUTHORITY OF HIS CHRIST HAVE COME, FOR THE ACCUSER OF OUR BRETHREN HAS BEEN THROWN DOWN, WHO ACCUSED THEM, DAY AND NIGHT BEFORE OUR GOD."

Satan must have been a thorn in the side of God, being before our God for all these thousands of years, accusing the brethren as he did in Job's day, and never ceasing to rail accusations before the throne.

When Simeon entered the temple, and when they brought the Baby Jesus to be circumcised he took the babe in his arms and said, "Now I have seen the salvation of the Lord, now let thy servant depart in peace".

Here Christ has been in heaven for over Two Thousand years, after his death and resurrection, has it taken all this time to destroy all Satan's power and authority in the heavens?

For it was after he was thrown out, that the Angels rejoiced for then their salvation had fully come, and so it will be on the earth, when Satan is fully defeated, then we will find our salvation for eternity has come.

This will be when all the saints are resurrected before God in heaven, crying out, "Salvation belongs to our God" Revelation Chapter 7 v 9-14, for these are they that have just passed through the great tribulation.

REVELATION CHAPTER 12 VERSES 11 - 12

SATAN'S REMOVAL FROM HEAVEN BRINGS JOY, BUT WOE TO THE EARTH.

Verse 11 "AND THEY HAVE CONQUERED HIM BY THE BLOOD OF THE LAMB AND BY THE WORD OF THEIR TESTIMONY, FOR THEY LOVED NOT THEIR LIVES EVEN UNTO DEATH."

Verses 12 "REJOICE THEN, O HEAVEN, AND YOU THAT DWELL THEREIN BUT WOE TO THE EARTH AND SEA, FOR THE DEVIL HAS COME DOWN TO YOU IN GREAT WRATH, BECAUSE HE KNOWS THAT HIS TIME IS SHORT."

Our faith in the blood of the lamb will not only sustain us in persecution, but assures us of life after death. Satan has lied and deceived the heavens for thousands of years and how long before creation was made, only our Lord can reveal. If one third of the angelic army, fighting with Satan, are cast out, it is then, when joy is finally experienced.

In the last world war, on V. E. Day, when victory had finally come, celebrations broke out, over most of world. This is the joy that heaven experiences, as we learn much from the latter times of verse 12, Satan's great wrath explodes on earth, beyond anything seen on earth up to now, The only good thing a Christian can say is that he has only to reign for three and a half years, or forty two months, This is the time of abomination, of desolation, when Satan's wrath is seen upon the earth.

We have seen the devastation he causes in Chapters 8 and 9, when he tried to destroy the world, before God shows him His wrath at the last day, when he obliterates his armies and destroys all who have the mark of the beast, or worship the image of the beast.

REVELATION CHAPTER 12 VERSES 13 - 14

SATAN'S PERSECUTION OF JEWISH CHRISTIANS IN ISRAEL ON ENTERING THE EARTH.

Verse 13 "AND WHEN THE DRAGON SAW HE HAD BEEN THROWN DOWN TO EARTH, HE PURSUED THE WOMAN, WHO HAD BORNE THE MALE CHILD."

Verse 14 "BUT THE WOMAN WAS GIVEN THE TWO WINGS OF A GREAT EAGLE THAT SHE MIGHT FLY FROM THE SERPENT INTO THE WILDERNESS, TO A PLACE WHERE SHE IS NOURISHED FOR A TIME, AND TIMES, AND HALF A TIME."

As we have said, the Woman represents the Christian Church in Israel, and Jerusalem, who have just had the first fruit of the Martyred saints swept into heaven who are to rule with Christ in the world to come. It is then that the Christians in Judea are warned to flee into the wilderness to a safe haven prepared by God.

He warned them in the following scriptures, from the Gospels, Matthew 24 verse 16 and again in Luke chapter 21 verse 21, speaking of end time he says 'then let those who are in Judea, flee to the mountains. Then in Mark Chapter 13 verse 14-20, again warns those in Judea to flee to the mountains.

In 2 Thessalonians chapter 2 verses 3-4, being in the temple in Jerusalem, as the man of sin the son of perdition, who opposes and exalts himself against every so called god, or object of worship so that he takes his seat in the temple of God proclaiming himself to be God, so God in heaven protects his church in Jerusalem in the wilderness for 42 months as in Daniel chapter 9 three and a half years, 1260 days, to the end of the great tribulation.

REVELATION CHAPTER 12 VERSES 15 - 17

GOD RESTRAIN'S SATAN'S ATTEMPT TO DECEIVE THOSE CHRISTIANS

Verse 15 "THE SERPENT POURED WATER LIKE A RIVER OUT OF HIS MOUTH AFTER THE WOMAN, TO SWEEP HER AWAY WITH THE FLOOD."

Verse 16 "BUT THE EARTH CAME TO HELP THE WOMAN, AND THE EARTH OPENED ITS MOUTH AND SWALLOWED THE RIVER WHICH THE DRAGON HAD POURED FROM HIS MOUTH."

Out of the mouth of the same Serpent in the Garden of Eden, came lies and deceit that caused Adam and Eve to sin by transgressing God's commandment. But, since then he has lost his heavenly power by being cast to the earth, God Supernaturally used this world to absorb and swallow up the river of lies that came from his mouth, he protected his Middle-Eastern Church in Judah, by warning them to flee into the wilderness. Again our Lord is in command in Satan's final hours in the world and he can only fulfil what God has written in the Bible especially in the book of Revelation. The Lord made cross references to this time, in various writings both in the Gospels and the Old Testament.

SATAN ATTACKS THE CHRISTIAN CHURCH WORLDWIDE.

Verse 17 "THEN THE DRAGON WAS ANGRY WITH THE WOMAN AND WENT OFF TO MAKE WAR ON THE REST OF HER OFFSPRING THOSE WHO KEEP THE COMMANDMENTS OF GOD AND BEAR TESTIMONY TO JESUS, AND HE STOOD ON THE SAND OF THE SEA."

Satan was very angry when his attempt to destroy those Christians in Judea and Jerusalem failed. They had responded to Gods call to flee, into the wilderness, which was spoken of in the Gospels (Luke 21-21 and Matt 24-16) Satan was so furious, he turns on Christians world wide. In the next Chapter we will see how he rises in the earth, and the methods by which he attacks the Christians in the rest of the world. Our Lord has left us all these prophetic scriptures to direct us and prepare us for what Satan is planning. We must always remember we are living in the last days, having the privilege to sacrifice our lives for our Saviour, just as he did for us.

REVELATION CHAPTER 13 VERSES 1 - 2

THE MYSTERY OF THE DRAGON, THE BEAST AND FALSE PROPHET

Verse 1 "AND I SAW A BEAST RISING OUT OF THE SEA, WITH TEN HORNS AND SEVEN HEADS, WITH TEN DIADEMS UPON ITS HORNS AND A BLASPHEMOUS NAME UPON ITS HEAD."

In Daniel, Chapter 7, verse.7 talking prophetically of end times we see Satan's power being given to the fourth beast, for it had 10 horns. These beasts at this time were all linked to the end of the world and the 4th one is referred to as terrible, dreadful, and exceedingly strong, it had great iron teeth. It devours and brakes in pieces, stamping the residue with its feet, so Satan who had so much power in heaven links with the beast, who had made a seven year peace agreement, in the Middle East and had great influence over 10 nations of the East.

All the preparation by the beast was in place when Satan was cast out of heaven, and took up his residence in Jerusalem. If you link this with the first four seals (Revelation Ch.6 v.7) you see the fourth rider of the horse was Satan, the Dragon who influences all the other riders in their destruction of the earth.

THE DRAGON IMPARTS HIS POWER TO THE BEAST WHO ACTS LIKE A FEROCIOUS ANIMAL.

Verse 2 "AND THE BEAST THAT I SAW WAS LIKE A LEOPARD. ITS FEET WERE LIKE A BEAR'S AND ITS MOUTH WAS LIKE A LION'S MOUTH AND TO IT THE DRAGON GAVE HIS POWER AND THE THRONE, AND GREAT AUTHORITY."

Here we have the Dragon, Satan giving his power to the beast. Satan is the God of this world who, when tempting Christ and showing him the glory of the nations, said to him "all this will I give you, if you worship me". When Satan imparts his power to the beast, he will become like a ferocious animal, just as Hitler during the last war. In fact, I believe he becomes ten thousand times worse.

You will remember, in Chapter nine, he destroys up to a third of the population of the world. In Daniel, Chapter.7 verses. 9 - 11, we see the beast's throne taken away when the ancient of days comes to take his seat. Christ comes at the end of the Beast's reign. The saints are judged for their deeds but the Beast was burnt up, its body destroyed. (In Hell)

REVELATION CHAPTER 13 VERSE 3 - 4

THE DRAGON, USED HIS HEALING POWER, TO BRING WORSHIP TO THE BEAST.

Verse 3 "ONE OF ITS HEADS SEEMED TO HAVE A MORTAL WOUND, BUT THE MORTAL WOUND WAS HEALED AND THE WHOLE EARTH FOLLOWED THE BEAST WITH WONDER. (**v4**) MEN WORSHIPPED THE DRAGON FOR HE HAD GIVEN HIS AUTHORITY TO THE BEAST, AND WORSHIPPED THE BEAST, SAYING "WHO IS LIKE THE BEAST, WHO CAN FIGHT AGAINST IT?"

There are many cults and religious sects who have certain evil powers which they use to deceive thousands of people to follow them, they worship their gods, i.e. demonic spirits which Our Lord cast out on many occasions. Paul came upon a woman who had a spirit of divination and he cast it out, in the name of Our Lord.

There are many cults such as the spiritualists with familiar spirits who deceive many to follow them. There are also many lying spirits and seducing spirits. Millions, like Islamic nations, and nearly all the eastern states, have fallen into Idol worship, then there are the communist countries, such as Russia, China, North Korea, who promote their people to be Atheists, not to believe there is a God.

Coming back to the text, Satan then healed the beast, who had been mortally wounded, and this one healing, brought worship to the Dragon and the Beast. Look at Jesus, healing thousands from every disease, yet at that time, most turned against him, rejecting him and even despising him, refusing to accept him as their Messiah, and Creator of the world. Instead of worshipping him, they crucified him. Our Lord even said that all in the graves shall be resurrected, the righteous to eternal life, the unrighteous eternal damnation, and we see this doctrine, happening many times in the book of Revelation.

REVELATION CHAPTER 13 VERSES 5 - 6

GOD ONLY ALLOWS SATAN A LIMITED TIME TO REIGN ON THE EARTH.

Verse 5 "AND THE BEAST WAS GIVEN A MOUTH, UTTERING HAUGHTY AND BLASPHEMOUS WORDS, AND IT WAS ALLOWED TO EXERCISE AUTHORITY FOR FORTY TWO MONTHS."

Verse 6 "IT OPENED ITS MOUTH TO UTTER BLASPHEMIES AGAINST GOD, BLASPHEMING HIS NAME AND HIS DWELLING THAT IS THOSE WHO DWELL IN HEAVEN."

Remember Satan has just been cast out of heaven and it is written "Woe unto the inhabitants of the earth for Satan is cast out knowing he only has but a short time". Daniel spoke of this in Chapter 9 v 27 "Satan will come with authority in Jerusalem in the midst of a seven year peace agreement". This being three and a half years, as Paul said in Thessalonians, Chapter 2, v. 4. "So he takes his seat in the temple of God, proclaiming himself, to be God".

This is the time of great tribulation, if these days were not shortened there would be no flesh saved, but for the Elects' sake these days will be shortened. When Our Lord was glorified with his Father receiving all knowledge, He reveals this book, and previous prophesies which will blend into Christ's revelation concerning the end times, so that every Christian has a perfect understanding as to what he must endure and pass through.

REVELATION CHAPTER 13 VERSE 7.

THE BEAST IS ALLOWED VICTORY OVER THE CHRISTIANS WORLDWIDE

Verse 7 "ALSO IT WAS ALLOWED TO MAKE WAR ON THE SAINTS TO CONQUER THEM, AND AUTHORITY WAS GIVEN IT, OVER EVERY TRIBE AND PEOPLE, TONGUE AND NATION."

The whole world must have been deceived by this man, named here as the Beast. When Satan is cast out of heaven, he completely takes him over by his power and manifests himself in him and through him, bonding together as one. He had gained authority in the whole world, so that he is able to persecute every saint. Then he must be accepted as a world leader with a league of nations, with a world currency ruling the world market, and finally he is a world dictator with world wide authority.

With this power, he turns the world against the saints of God on the earth, i.e. he has the power to persecute them. Every Christian saint has this promise of God, that if they suffer with Christ, they will also reign with him. Remember the resurrection comes at the end of the three and a half years. Also, we have the promise given by our Lord, as written in John Ch.11-v.25, Jesus said "I am the resurrection and the life, he that believes in me though he die, yet shall he live, and whosoever lives and believes in me, shall NEVER die." This means our spirit and soul ascends to heaven at death, and only one part, our body goes to the grave, awaiting the resurrection at the coming of Christ.

When I was studying the seven foundation truths, I spent over two years on anthropology, 'Body, Soul, and Spirit' from an Oxford Lecturer, and Chaplain, one of the most educated men, who taught in the Pentecostal Bible College in the early 1930's, and like Moses, he suffered the reproaches of men, denying himself the riches of this world, for the Lords work and for the Lords sake.

REVELATION CHAPTER 13 VERSES 8 - 9

ONLY THOSE WHOSE NAMES ARE WRITTEN IN THE LAMB'S BOOK OF LIFE, WILL OVERCOME SATAN.

Verse 8 "AND ALL THOSE WHO DWELL ON EARTH WILL WORSHIP IT, EVERY ONE WHO'S NAME HAS NOT BEEN WRITTEN BEFORE THE FOUNDATION OF THE WORLD, IN THE BOOK OF LIFE OF THE LAMB THAT WAS SLAIN."

Verse 9 "IF ANY ONE HAS AN EAR, LET HIM HEAR."

This verse again has caused some saints to come to two doctrines, some say God has a purpose before the foundation of the world, that some people are going to heaven, others are destined for hell, and its God's prerogative to choose who goes where. I have studied both opinions and I believe the second, is true, God planned and purposed Christ to come into the world to save the world of Sinners, the bible say's 'faith comes by hearing', hearing of the word of God. Then it is written, 'how shall they hear without a preacher?' The commission of Christ was, 'go ye into all the world, and preach the gospel'. They that believe shall be saved, they that do not believe shall be damned. Every one has a free will, and is responsible of either accepting Christ as Saviour, or rejecting him.

When John the Baptist saw Jesus walking, he said "Behold the Lamb of God that takes away the sin of the world" In Revelation Ch.12 "and they overcame the Devil when cast onto earth, by the blood of the Lamb, and by the word of their testimony." There are many other scriptures which need to be examined, only a few servants have exercised their minds to know right from wrong, so let us have ears to hear, and a heart to understand. I thank God that he brought me to true repentance, again, it is written 'Unless a man repent, he will perish'.

The moment I called out to the Lord, he saved me, like Paul who was persecuting God's children, yet he turned, in true repentance and followed Christ.

REVELATION CHAPTER 13 VERSE 10

OUR CHRISTIAN FAITH, AT THIS TIME, WILL BE TESTED, TO THE VERY LIMIT.

Verse 10 "IF ANY ONE IS TAKEN CAPTIVE, TO CAPTIVITY HE GOES, IF ANY ONE SLAYS WITH THE SWORD, BY THE SWORD HE WILL BE SLAIN.HERE IS A CALL FOR THE ENDURANCE AND FAITH OF THE SAINTS.

In Matthew Chapter 24 verse.9, "Then they will deliver you up to tribulation and put you to death and you will be hated by all nations for my name's sake". So Christians are continually warned of this time of great tribulation and if those days are not shortened there could be no flesh saved, but for the elect's sake those days will be shortened to 42 months.

Christians have no idea what is coming to the earth. The endurance and persecution we have to face when Satan is cast out of heaven, having great wrath, when a third of the population will perish, 2.2 Billion, and also the billions who take his mark and worship him.

We have one great consolation, to be absent from the body is to be present with the Lord, and for many of the elect, these days will be shortened. This means Our Lord is going to sweep us into Glory.

We are told that we cannot battle or fight our way out of the devilish power of persecution, but he that endures till the end, shall be saved. This will be a testing time for our faith.

REVELATION CHAPTER 13 VERSES 11 - 12

THE THIRD MEMBER OF SATAN'S SYNDICATE IS REVEALED ON EARTH

Verse 11 "THEN I SAW ANOTHER BEAST WHICH ROSE OUT OF THE EARTH; IT HAD TWO HORNS LIKE A LAMB, AND IT SPOKE LIKE A DRAGON."

Verse 12 "IT EXERCISES ALL THE AUTHORITY OF THE FIRST BEAST IN ITS PRESENCE, AND MAKES THE EARTH AND ITS INHABITANTS WORSHIP THE FIRST BEAST WHOSE MORTAL WOUND WAS HEALED."

This beast that also arose out of one of the nations is known as the false Prophet, he exercises the power of Satan, so that the spirit within him is a devilish one and he brings the inhabitants of the world to worship the first beast.

As Adolph Hitler arose looking harmless but soon showed his true colours, then 50 Million died, because of his authority and power in the nation of Germany. This beast comes on the scene at the same time as the first beast who was healed. It appears he has worldwide influence and authority and seduces the world to worship the beast as the Devil himself sought worship in heaven and all the Angels in heaven who did worship him, fought for him. This Beast, and false prophet, use their power worldwide.

The amazing revelation God has given through John the apostle, has shown every Christian the steps that Satan will take upon the earth, so that every Christian can understand the events that Satan is about to accomplish upon the earth, and that we are on the winning side and will live with Christ for ever. (Amen)

REVELATION CHAPTER 13 VERSES 13 - 15

THE SIGNS AND WONDERS GOD ALLOWS THE FALSE PROPHET TO ACCOMPLISH

Verse 13 "IT WORKS GREAT SIGNS, EVEN MAKING FIRE COME DOWN FROM HEAVEN TO EARTH IN THE SIGHT OF MEN. (**v14**) BY THESE SIGNS WHICH IT IS ALLOWED TO WORK IN THE PRESENCE OF THE BEAST, IT DECEIVED THOSE WHO DWELT ON EARTH, BIDDING THEM MAKE AN IMAGE FOR THE BEAST, WHICH WAS WOUNDED BY THE SWORD, AND YET LIVED. (**v15**) IT WAS ALLOWED TO GIVE BREATH TO THE IMAGE OF THE BEAST SO THAT THE IMAGE OF THE BEAST SHOULD EVEN SPEAK AND CAUSE THOSE WHO WOULD NOT WORSHIP THE IMAGE OF THE BEAST TO BE SLAIN."

The Lord, when banishing Satan from heaven, still allowed him to retain certain powers so that he can fulfil His Word, but still holds him responsible for his actions even as our law condemns any person for breaking the law, not blaming the mother or father but just the man himself, as Ezekiel Chapter 18 explains this truth plus other scriptures which confirm this point. Satan had great power when he attacked Job, and he has influenced many to operate his powers, such as astrologers, wizards, magicians, fortune tellers, spiritualists, and many more. These powers are operated to bring glory to oneself as Satan did in heaven, when finding himself on earth, he uses his power through his two associates to convince the world to worship him, then he works another incredible feat to bring the world to worship him, this time he makes an image of the beast, and breaks two of the first commandments.

Never in past history, has an image been made, that is able to speak, but we must remember, we are in the age of computers and Satan is no ordinary person, but has powers and is able to programme it to his own mind and ways and convince the world to worship him and to slay any person who will not worship him or receive his mark. Again he has the power world-wide to execute Christians who refuse to worship him, even now the world seems to be heading for a one world government, one monetary fund, and one dictator, I am sure all these things will happen in the next few years. To a Christian, death is just the start of a new life, as Paul says "to be absent from the body is to be present with our Lord" In John, it says "They that believe in me shall never die" do you believe this?. So as Christians, let us take hold of the promises of our Almighty God.

REVELATION CHAPTER 13 VERSES 16 - 18

SATAN FORCES THE WORLD TO RECEIVE HIS MARK, TO BE ABLE TO PURCHASE FOOD.

Verse 16 "IT CAUSES ALL BOTH SMALL AND GREAT, BOTH RICH AND POOR, BOTH SLAVE AND FREE, TO BE MARKED ON THE RIGHT HAND OR THE FOREHEAD. (**v17**) SO THAT NO ONE CAN BUY OR SELL UNLESS HE HAS HIS MARK, THAT IS, THE NAME OF THE BEAST, OR THE NUMBER OF ITS NAME. (**v18**) THIS CALLS FOR WISDOM, LET HIM WHO HAS UNDERSTANDING, RECKON THE NUMBER OF THE BEAST, FOR IT IS A HUMAN NUMBER, IT IS SIX HUNDRED AND SIXTY SIX."

Another amazing power he has, in the world, is to be able to put his number on every person, in villages in towns and cities. This is an incredible feat, throughout the world, no one has ever achieved anything like it. Also, he has the power to prevent any person from buying or selling without his mark, but as Christians know, we do not live by bread alone.

If our God can provide for two to three million people for forty years in the wilderness, and in the New-Testament feed five thousand, and seven thousand with a few loaves and fishes, then he can feed us. We have been promised in Daniel that they that know their God, shall be strong, and do exploits, so too, for all who believe, God will supply their needs according to his riches in Glory. Remember the cattle on a thousand hills are His.

At this time, all the food in the world is going to be under the Devil's control. This dictator is going to rule the world by the fear, of himself. He is trying to prove he is the god of this world. But, our God is only allowing him forty two months, just a limited time, as He said in verse five, of this chapter.

REVELATION CHAPTER 14

Introduction

WE WILL DIVIDE THE FOLLOWING CHAPTER, INTO THREE MAIN HEADINGS.

1. verses 1-5 THE MYSTERY OF THE ONE HUNDRED AND FORTY-FOUR THOUSAND (over comers) WITH CHRIST.

2. Verses 6-11 THE THREE ANGELIC REVALATIONS TO BE PREACHED ON EARTH.

3. verses 12-20 GOD'S TWO REAPINGS OF THE RIGHTEOUS AND THE UNRIGHTEOUS ON THE LAST DAY.

REVELATION CHAPTER 14 VERSES 1 - 3

THE MYSTERY OF THE ONE HUNDRED AND FORTY FOUR THOUSAND OVER COMERS WITH CHRIST.

Verse 1 “THEN I LOOKED AND LO, ON MOUNT ZION STOOD THE LAMB, WITH HIM A HUNDRED AND FORTY FOUR THOUSAND WHO HAD HIS NAME, AND HIS FATHER'S NAME WRITTEN ON THEIR FOREHEADS. (**v2**) AND I HEARD A VOICE FROM HEAVEN LIKE THE SOUND OF MANY WATERS, AND LIKE THE SOUND OF THUNDER,

THE VOICE I HEARD WAS LIKE THE SOUND OF HARPISTS PLAYING ON THEIR HARPS. **(v3)** THEY SANG A NEW SONG BEFORE THE THRONE, BEFORE THE FOUR LIVING CREATURES AND BEFORE THE ELDERS. NO-ONE CAN LEARN THAT SONG EXCEPT THE HUNDRED AND FORTY-FOUR THOUSAND WHO HAD BEEN REDEEMED FROM THE EARTH."

I believe this contingent of a hundred and forty four thousand are standing in heaven before the Lamb of God and accompanying them, an orchestra of Angel's playing songs specially composed for these saints, who are redeemed. If we look at the tabernacle in the wilderness given to Moses, it was a replica of the original one in Heaven, so it looks as if Mount Zion is in heaven.

They are before the throne with the Lamb of God and the four cherubs and twenty four Elders, No-one else will be able to sing this song, for they have achieved a sanctification above those who are redeemed from the earth.

REVELATION CHAPTER 14 VERSES 4 - 5

THE STANDARD OF SANCTIFICATION REQUIRED TO SING THIS SONG.

Verse 4 "IT IS THOSE WHO HAVE NOT DEFILED THEMSELVES WITH WOMEN, FOR THEY ARE CHASTE, IT IS FOR THESE WHO FOLLOW THE LAMB WHERE-EVER HE GOES, THESE HAVE BEEN REDEEMED FROM MANKIND AS FIRST FRUITS FOR GOD AND FOR THE LAMB."

Verse 5 "IN THEIR MOUTH, NO LIE WAS FOUND, FOR THEY ARE SPOTLESS."

Woman was made from the rib of man, made for man, and it was Eve, that was first tempted to sin. Job would not allow his wife to influence him, when under a direct assault from the Devil; he refused his wife's words to curse God and die.

Every Man, like King David, has been tempted at some time, by a woman, to sin. Only these few from all the earth can sing this song. There are many good women of faith who have risen to be mentioned in the Bible for their love for God, i.e. Rahab, Ruth, Mary and many more.

These two verses show sanctification on earth is rewarded in heaven. Our Lord said Obedience is better than sacrifice, every Christian is allowed by God to be tempted Our Lord was tempted at all points as we are, yet without sin, so these one hundred and forty four thousand have been tempted and have come through spotless they have overcome like their Lord, the spotless Lamb of God.

These saints are referred to as the first fruits, they are special among the saints and are rewarded by being allowed in heaven to walk with the Lord. The greatness of this testing is, if we are able to pass through with flying colours, then we will become a reflection of our Lord, in character.

REVELATION CHAPTER 14 VERSES 6 - 7

THE FIRST OF GOD'S THREE ANGELS, REVEALING MYSTERIES OF THE END TIMES

Verse 6 "THEN I SAW ANOTHER ANGEL FLYING IN MID HEAVEN WITH AN ETERNAL GOSPEL TO PROCLAIM TO THOSE WHO DWELL ON EARTH."

Verse 7 "AND HE SAID WITH A LOUD VOICE "FEAR GOD AND GIVE HIM GLORY, FOR THE HOUR OF HIS JUDGEMENT HAS COME, AND WORSHIP HIM WHO MADE HEAVEN AND EARTH, THE SEA, AND THE FOUNTAINS OF WATER."

The first of the three angels all with special messages, is flying across the world ensuring that before the end of the world, the gospel is preached throughout all nations. This was the last commandment given to Christ's disciples, (in Mark Ch.16 v. 15).This Angel is seeing this commandment is finally carried out. The next revelation is God's judgement which will only come as the gospel is proclaimed throughout all nations. He also reveals that God's judgement only comes when all prophetic scripture is fulfilled.

In Revelation Ch. 10 v 7 the day of the seventh trumpet the mystery of God announced by his prophets will be fulfilled again. Another scripture talking of end times at Christ's coming, is Revelation Ch 11 v 18 where it says the nations raged but thy wrath is come and the time for the dead to be judged for the rewarding of thy servants, the prophet and saints and those that fear thy name both small and great, then he goes on to say, that on the same day, wrath will be poured out on that day he will destroy those who are destroying the earth.

This will happen at the battle of Armageddon, when he destroys the armies of Satan, i.e. 200 million also every person in the world who has the mark of the beast. This will run into billions. The same day that Noah entered the Ark and was saved, the inhabitants of the world perished. Christ spoke of his coming in the gospels, he also said that the same day Lot came out of Sodom, fire destroyed the city, and this truth runs all the way through this book.

REVELATION CHAPTER 14 VERSE 8

THE MYSTERY OF THE SECOND ANGEL'S REVELATION

Verse 8 "ANOTHER ANGEL, A SECOND FOLLOWED, SAYING "FALLEN, FALLEN, IS BABYLON THE GREAT, SHE WHO MADE ALL NATIONS DRINK THE WINE OF HER IMPURE PASSION."

This place, Babylon, has been a mystery to many expositors, many have written their suggestions so that Christians are confused with so many conflicting views. The book of Revelation from Chapter four, to twenty is describing the events of the last forty two months, One thousand two hundred and sixty days, the last three and a half years.

Daniel had spoken in Chapter 9 v 27, when Gabriel talked of the last three and a half years of the seven year peace agreement, when the abomination of desolation spoken of by our Lord, which he referred to in Matthew Ch 24 v 29 regarding Christ's coming again.

It is after our Lord was glorified with his father when he became equal and regained all power to reveal to John everything relating to end times. Coming back to this Angel's revelation of Babylon, I personally believe after approximately 25 years of study that Babylon is Jerusalem.

There are so many scriptures to support this personal view, some I have mentioned in the previous chapters, which I will recapitulate, but, first in Matthew ch.23 v 34-37, Jerusalem was the place God sent his prophets, wise men, and scribes, some they killed, some they crucified, others they scourged from town to town, all the blood from Abel to Zechariah shall come upon them.

Then our Lord said, "O Jerusalem, Jerusalem, killing the prophet and stoning those who are sent unto you! How I would have gathered your children together as a hen gathers her brood under her wings, and you would not. Behold your house is forsaken and desolate, for I tell you, you will not see me again until you say, blessed is he who comes in the name of the Lord".

Remember after this our Lord was crucified at Jerusalem, then his disciples were persecuted, killed, and scattered all over the world, they were also killed in many other countries, it is estimated 250,000 Christians are still being martyred for their faith in Christ each year. Remember this, as I will bring more on this as we examine Revelation chapters 17 and 18.

We read in both Revelation Ch.12 and in 2 Thessalonians ch.2 v. 4, that when Satan is cast out of heaven, he takes his place in the temple in Jerusalem, showing himself as God, this was his original desire; this was spoken to us in Ezekiel Chapter 28.

Going back to Jerusalem, God allowed His two prophets to be killed by him, Revelation ch.11 v. 8-9, then raised them in their bodies which had laid in the street for three days. At that time, he referred to Jerusalem as 'that great city called Sodom and Egypt the place where our Lord was crucified'. And the last battle, the battle of Armageddon is in and around Jerusalem.

It is at this time, when the people of Jerusalem will call upon the name of the Lord, then he will come and save a remnant, 144,000,(as many have already fled into the wilderness to God's Haven, Revelation Ch.12, V.6) and he will rebuild Jerusalem, which will last a thousand years, before creating a new earth and a new heaven, with a new heavenly City which will be revealed later in the book.

REVELATION CHAPTER 14 VERSES 9 - 10

THE THIRD ANGEL REVEALS THAT ANYONE WORSHIPPING THE BEAST WILL COME UNDER GOD'S WRATH

Verse 9 "AND ANOTHER ANGEL A THIRD, FOLLOWED THEM SAYING WITH A LOUD VOICE, "IF ANYONE WORSHIP'S THE BEAST AND ITS IMAGE, AND RECEIVES A MARK UPON HIS FOREHEAD OR ON HIS HAND, (**v10**) HE ALSO SHALL DRINK THE WINE OF GOD'S WRATH, POURED UNMIXED INTO THE CUP OF HIS ANGER, AND HE SHALL BE TORMENTED WITH FIRE AND SUPHUR IN THE PRESENCE OF HOLY ANGELS AND IN THE PRESENCE OF THE LAMB".

This third Angel is referring to Chapter 13, when the devil links with his earthly associates, the beast and the false prophet, these three work together as one; when we see the beast we also see the devil. Christians must not be deceived, as the consequence for not worshipping the beast and his image, or receiving his mark, is death. But look at the judgement of God's wrath, which is poured into the cup of his anger. The anger and wrath of God do not come, until after Satan rules, during the forty two month period which is called the great tribulation, when God allows him his final assault on the earth. Before this time, God has allowed every nation to hear the gospel of the saving grace of his son Jesus Christ, and they have refused him. So God has promised them that his wrath will be poured out on them at the end. This judgement comes at the end of Satan's reign. It is a judgment of hell fire and eternal banishment, it is an eternal punishment, as fire and sulphur burns, so their souls will suffer, which is the eternal part of man that cannot be destroyed.

God will not allow their souls to have a body and enjoy life in God's creation any more. He explains this judgment in the gospel saying "where the worm dies not, and the fire is not quenched" I was privileged to study the book of C L Parker who taught the seven foundation in the Pentecostal Bible College in the 1930's One of his subjects was Anthropology, the teaching on Body, Soul and Spirit, of Man. I personally went into the Bible College at Mattersey in the 1970's and found they had no understanding of his teaching. I am so glad I have embraced his teaching and understood it, as it laid a good foundation in me. Another scripture which I use for understanding this truth is "Fear not them that can kill the body, but cannot kill the soul, but fear him that can cast body and soul into hell." It is then that fire and sulphur will destroy the body, but the soul will live on in torment, for eternity, the fire in their soul is not quenched.

REVELATION CHAPTER 14 VERSES 11 - 13

THIS JUDGMENT EXECUTED BY OUR GOD WILL LAST THROUGHOUT ETERNITY.

Verse 11 "AND THE SMOKE OF THEIR TORMENT GOES UP FOREVER AND EVER, AND THEY HAVE NO REST, DAY AND NIGHT, THESE WORSHIPPERS OF THE BEAST AND ITS IMAGE, AND WHOSOEVER RECEIVES THE MARK OF ITS NAME."

So this judgement of God lasts forever. Think of it, they have no rest for their soul without a body, the realisation of never having another body is torment, but this is the only way God can stop iniquity and ungodliness. This is the only course of action open to God to stop sin and remove it from the world to come. Man has had the opportunity of accepting the truth of the Son, who gave his life for their sins and they have refused. They had the opportunity of not only being called a son of God, but also being transformed daily and being changed into the image of His Son.

GOD WARNS CHRISTIANS THAT THEY MAY FACE DEATH BEFORE THE END.

Verse 12 "HERE IS A CALL FOR ENDURANCE OF THE SAINTS, THOSE WHO KEEP THE COMMANDMENTS OF GOD AND THE FAITH OF JESUS. (**v13**) AND I HEARD A VOICE FROM HEAVEN SAYING "WRITE THIS; BLESSED ARE THE DEAD WHO DIE IN THE LORD, HENCEFORTH" "BLESSED INDEED" SAYS THE SPIRIT, "THAT THEY MAY REST FROM THEIR LABOURS, FOR THEIR DEEDS FOLLOW THEM!""

This verse shows that Christians must be ready to sacrifice their lives for our Lord. We are just reflecting the love of God in us. We remember death is just the beginning of life in heaven, as Paul said, "To be absent from the body is to be present with the Lord". We are also obeying his commandment, not to worship any other god or graven image, but only Jesus, our Lord. Christians have endured suffering throughout their lifetime, when Satan finds himself on the earth; he intensifies suffering in every nation. But here our Lord is inspiring us with the truth that to die is gain; we are blessed indeed to be able to rest in heaven. It is in Heaven that we receive our rewards, as Revelation Chapter 11 v. 15 -18 states. This is referring to the Christians' Resurrection and our rewards, as the Spirit also says "that we may rest from our labour, and our works and deed, follow us." Remember God allows the Devil to fulfil all these prophetic verses at the end times, like destroying lands, polluting water systems, and killing up to a third of the population of the world. God still holds him responsible for his evil actions.

REVELATION CHAPTER 14 VERSES 14 - 16

GOD'S TWO REAPINGS OF THE RIGHTEOUS AND THE UNRIGHTEOUS.

In the next few verses we see the reaping of the righteous into heaven, and at the same time, we see the reaping of the unrighteous who are destroyed in Hell.

CHRIST COMES FIRST TO REAP HIS CHURCH.

Verse 14 "THEN I LOOKED, AND LO A WHITE CLOUD, AND SEATED ON THE CLOUD, ONE LIKE A SON OF MAN, WITH A GOLDEN CROWN ON HIS HEAD AND A SHARP SICKLE IN HIS HAND." **(v15)** ANOTHER ANGEL CAME OUT OF THE TEMPLE, CALLING WITH A LOUD VOICE, TO HIM WHO SAT UPON THE CLOUD, " PUT IN YOUR SICKLE, AND REAP, FOR THE HOUR TO REAP

HAS NOW COME , FOR THE HARVEST OF THE EARTH IS FULLY RIPE, (**v16**) SO HE WHO SAT ON THE CLOUD, SWUNG HIS SICKLE ON THE EARTH, AND THE EARTH WAS REAPED."

When our Lord ascended into heaven and the cloud received him out of sight, two angels appeared and said "This same Jesus who was taken up from you into Heaven, will come in the same way". Another scripture in this context was when Jesus spoke of the good seed and the tares. He said "let them remain together until the end, lest you reap the good up with bad." They were separated at the end of time. Also in Matthew 24 v.29-31 immediately after the tribulation, after the devil destroyed as much of the earth as God allows him, then Christ will come in the clouds of Heaven and he will send his Angels and they will gather his elect from the four winds, from one end of heaven to the other. The rest of the tribes of the earth will mourn, as they see their destiny.

All prophetic scripture links together so perfectly with the book of Revelation, it fits so easily like a jig-saw, revealing what our Lord wants us to understand of the end times. These two reapings happen on the same day. 2 Thessalonians, Ch.1 v 6-10, "since indeed God deems it just to repay with affliction those who afflict you, (v.7) and to grant rest with us to you who are afflicted, when the Lord Jesus is revealed from heaven with his mighty Angel's in flaming fire (v.8) inflicting vengeance upon those who do not obey the gospel of our Lord Jesus (v.9) they shall suffer the punishment of Eternal Destruction, and exclusion from the presence of the Lord and from the glory of his might". Then note - (v.10). "When he comes on that day, to be glorified in his saints, and to be marvelled at among all who believe", so, the day of the resurrection of the saints, is the day of the wrath of God.

REVELATION CHAPTER 14 VERSES 17 - 20

THE REAPING OF THE SAINT'S, AND THE WRATH OF GOD, ON THE UNGODLY HAPPEN ON THE SAME DAY OF THE LORD'S COMING.

Verse 17 "AND ANOTHER ANGEL CAME OUT OF THE TEMPLE IN HEAVEN. AND HE TOO HAD A SHARP SICKLE. (**v18**) THEN ANOTHER ANGEL CAME OUT FROM THE ALTAR, THE ANGEL WHO HAS POWER OVER FIRE, AND HE CALLED OUT WITH A LOUD VOICE TO HIM WHO HAD THE SHARP SICKLE, "PUT IN YOUR SICKLE AND GATHER THE CLUSTERS OF THE VINE OF THE EARTH FOR ITS GRAPES ARE RIPE" (**v19**) SO THE ANGEL SWUNG HIS SICKLE ON THE EARTH AND GATHERED THE VINTAGE OF THE EARTH AND THREW IT INTO THE GREAT WINEPRESS OF THE WRATH OF GOD. (**v20**) AND THE WINE PRESS WAS TRODDEN OUTSIDE THE CITY, AND BLOOD FLOWED FROM THE WINE PRESS, AS HIGH AS A HORSE'S BRIDLE FOR ONE THOUSAND, SIX HUNDRED FURLONGS."

This happens on the same day, that he takes his church to Glory, when all the dead in Christ shall arise from the grave, and they that are alive shall meet him in the air, ever to be with the Lord. We had a similar account in Revelation Ch 11 v. 18 at the end of the seventh trumpet, it says " The nations raged, but their wrath came, and the time of the dead to be judged for the rewarding of the saints and the prophets, and for destroying the destroyers of the earth, again in the sixth seal, Revelation Ch.6 v.16-17 we read, "fall on us and hide us from the face of him who is seated on the throne, and from the wrath of the Lamb, (V.17) For the great day of their wrath has come and who can stand".

Chapter 16 v.15-16 After the seventh plague, we have the final battle of Armageddon, and they all speak of the resurrection of the saints. Why expositors have tried to fit the Glorified Christ's teaching and the teaching of the apostle into the Old Testament prophets, instead of fitting them into Christ's teaching of the end times, I do not know. After all power and glory was rightly restored to the Lord, in the books of Revelation, so we are prepared against all that is written of the Devil. Every event which comes to pass is sanctioned within the temple in heaven, All this vast army, gathered by 10 nations of the east, comes into Israel, as God leads them into the wine-press of the wrath of God. Our Lord even tells us of the amount of Blood and the distance throughout Israel it will flow, this being the height of a horses bridle, for 1,600 furlongs.

Here I would like to bring in a couple of prophesies from the old testament which fits into Christ's teaching, found here; **JOEL Chapter 3 verses 9 - 16,**

Verse 9 PROCLAIM THIS AMONG THE NATIONS. PREPARE WAR, STIR UP THE MIGHTY MEN. LET ALL MEN OF WAR DRAW NEAR, LET THEM COME UP.

Verse 10 BEAT YOUR PLOWSHARES INTO SWORDS AND YOUR PRUNING HOOKS INTO SPEARS, LET THE WEAK SAY "I AM A WARRIOR".

Verse 11 HASTEN AND COME ALL YOU NATIONS ROUND ABOUT, GATHER YOURSELVES THERE. BRING DOWN THY WARRIORS, O LORD.

Verse 12 LET THE NATIONS BE AWAKENED, AND COME TO THE VALLEY OF JEHOSHAPHAT, FOR THERE I WILL SIT TO JUDGE ALL THE NATIONS ROUND ABOUT.

Verse 13 PUT IN THE SICKLE FOR THE HARVEST IS RIPE, GO IN, TREAD, FOR THE WINE PRESS IS FULL. THE VATS OVERFLOW, FOR THEIR WICKEDNESS IS GREAT.

Verse 14 MULTITUDES, MULTITUDES, IN THE VALLEY OF DECISION, FOR THE DAY OF THE LORD IS NEAR, IN THE VALLEY OF DECISION.

Verse 15 THE SUN AND THE MOON SHALL BE DARKENED, AND THE STARS SHALL WITHDRAW THEIR SHINING.

Verse 16 THE LORD ROARS FROM ZION, AND UTTERS HIS VOICE FROM JERUSALEM, AND THE HEAVENS AND EARTH WILL SHAKE. BUT THE LORD WILL BE A REFUGE TO HIS PEOPLE, A STRONG HOLD TO THE PEOPLE OF ISRAEL.

The next scripture referring to this chapter is found in **Zechariah**, Chapter 14, actually the whole of the chapter, fits into the signs to Christ's second coming, but I am only considering a couple of verses, 3-4 then verse 12.

<u>Verse 3</u> "THEN THE LORD WILL GO FORTH, AND FIGHT AGAINST THOSE NATIONS, AS HE FOUGHT ON THE DAY OF BATTLE. **(v4)** ON THAT DAY, HIS FEET SHALL STAND ON THE MOUNT OF OLIVES WHICH LIES BEFORE JERUSALEM ON THE EAST; AND THE MOUNT OF OLIVES SHALL BE SPLIT IN TWO FROM EAST TO WEST BY A VERY WIDE VALLEY, SO THAT ONE HALF OF THE MOUNTAIN SHALL WITHDRAW NORTHWARD, AND THE OTHER HALF SOUTHWARD."

This gives us a picture of this vast army of 200 Million, and how the Lord will kill them all by the brightness of his coming, remembering that this vast army was responsible for the death of a third of the population of the world, by fire and brimstone and smoke, and probably by nuclear missiles. People would dissolve.

Our Lord is a just God with a Just Judgement, so the Lord destroys this army with the same destruction, as we read of them in **Zechariah** chapter 14 verse 12 -

<u>Verse 12</u> "AND THE PLAGUE WITH WHICH THE LORD WILL SMITE ALL THE PEOPLE THAT WAGE WAR <u>AGAINST JERUSALEM</u>, THEIR FLESH SHALL ROT WHILE THEY STAND ON THEIR FEET, THEIR EYES SHALL ROT IN THEIR SOCKETS, AND THEIR TONGUES SHALL ROT IN THEIR MOUTHS."

So the blood of this vast army of 200 million assembled against Jerusalem at the battle of Armageddon will flow, and their blood will run down like a river, as deep as the bridle of a horse, for the distance of one thousand six hundred furlongs. Also at this same time, God judges all the world, who have received anti-christ's mark, and worshipped him, and any person who is saved at this time will come up to the New Jerusalem, to worship the Lord.

I am sure that many expositors, will be able to link many more scriptures with the book of Revelation, I only hope and pray the Lord will open up the Truth of his Word, as the day will declare who is right, or wrong. *(AMEN)*

REVELATION CHAPTER 15 VERSES 1 - 4

Introduction

Here we have another mystery in Heaven, of seven Angels, with the seven last plagues, to pour out on all who worship the Beast, his image, who have his number, all who have been deceived by the Devil. These plagues are also the wrath of God and the last plague ends the same day the Lord returns, so this chapter reveals what is happening both in heaven, and upon the earth at the end of the Great Tribulation.

THE MYSTERY IN HEAVEN OF THE SEVEN ANGELS WITH THE SEVEN LAST PLAGUES

Verse 1 "THEN I SAW, ANOTHER PORTENT IN HEAVEN, GREAT AND WONDERFUL, SEVEN ANGEL'S WITH SEVEN PLAGUES, WHICH ARE THE LAST, FOR WITH THEM, THE WRATH OF GOD IS ENDED."

There are so many ministering angels in the book of Revelation that the only way of identifying them, is by their ministry. If we look at the ministries on earth, there are thousands who minister God's word, yet they all pass into eternity, but the word of the Lord abides forever. These plagues end on God's final day, when the last of his wrath is poured out. If we remember, at the end of the 6th.Seal, in Revelation 6, v. 16-17 it says, "Fall on us, and hide us from the face of him who is seated on the throne (Christ) and from the Wrath of the Lamb, for the great day of their wrath has come".

Again as you read of the 7th trumpets in Revelation Ch.11 v 15-18 it states, "Christ has come to reign with great power." The Nations raged but thy wrath is come. Then in the last ch.14 v.19, "So the angel swung his sickle on the earth, and gathered the vintage of the earth, and threw it into the great wine-press of the wrath of God". All of the book of Revelation from Chapter 4 to Chapter 20, is talking of the same period of time, the last 42 months, or three and a half years, which is the period called the Great Tribulation. When Christ first came, many scriptures referred to his three and a half years' ministry. There were other scriptures concerning his birth, his time in Egypt and his return to Nazareth, but the vast majority speak of his ministry, his death, his resurrection, his ascension. He only allows the Devil three and a half years to reign, before his second coming, when he arrives to put down all of the Devil's power. Jesus must sit at his Fathers side until the earth becomes his footstool.

THE MYSTERY OF THE PERSECUTED SAINTS WHO HAVE PASSED INTO HEAVEN.

Verse 2 "AND I SAW WHAT APPEARED TO BE A SEA OF GLASS MINGLED WITH FIRE, AND THOSE WHO HAD CONQUERED THE BEAST AND IT'S IMAGE, AND THE NUMBER OF IT'S NAME, STANDING BESIDE THE SEA OF GLASS, WITH HARPS OF GOLD IN THEIR HANDS."

These are a few of the whole body of believers who suffered persecution and were martyred at the end times. These have been given harps to play on as they worship before the Lamb. We also see that they are before God's throne, as the same sea of glass was mentioned in Chapter 4, v. 6. A sea of glass, like crystal. Then in the 5th seal Chapter 6, V 9 ,if you remember, there were other souls martyred for Jesus, and these were presented with robes to wear, when the resurrection of their bodies take place.

ALL THE SAINTS UNITE IN SONG FROM THE OLD AND NEW TESTAMENTS

Verse 3 "THEY SING THE SONG OF MOSES, THE SERVANT OF GOD AND THE SONG OF THE LAMB SAYING "GREAT AND

WONDERFUL ARE THY DEEDS O LORD GOD ALMIGHTY! JUST AND TRUE ARE THY WAYS, O KING OF THE AGES!"

Verse 4 "WHO SHALL NOT FEAR AND GLORIFY THY NAME O LORD? FOR THOU ALONE ART HOLY, ALL NATIONS SHALL COME AND WORSHIP THEE, FOR THY JUDGMENTS HAVE BEEN REVEALED."

The lyrics of the song reveal that from Moses to Christ, the Lamb; from the servants in the Old Testament to Sons in the New Testament, they both unite in the same worship songs to God the Almighty. This embraces both old and new Testament believers, of the same faith, God is worshipped in many ways, being just, and true in all His ways, from the beginning of time to the end of time. He is always the same. He is a God who changes not. "Thou art worthy of all praise, all shall fear him and glorify thy name O Lord" For he was, he is, and ever shall be, The Almighty.

In the last line of the song, they refer to judgments which are to be revealed, these being the seven plagues which continue through to the end of Chapter 16 when the last battle to be recorded takes place, the battle of Armageddon. This is when Christ comes, and destroys Satan, the beast, the false prophet, and Their army.

REVELATION CHAPTER 15 VERSES 5 - 7

THE MYSTERY OF THE TEMPLE IN HEAVEN

Verse 5 "AFTER THIS I LOOKED AND THE TEMPLE OF THE TENT OF WITNESS IN HEAVEN WAS OPENED, **V.6** AND OUT OF THE TEMPLE CAME THE SEVEN ANGELS WITH SEVEN PLAGUES, ROBED IN PURE WHITE BRIGHT LINEN AND THEIR BREASTS GIRDED WITH GOLDEN GIRDLES."

This temple in heaven is the command centre of activity, simply because Jesus is our Great High Priest, who went into the temple in heaven with his own blood, and sits at his Father's right hand until the earth becomes his footstool. It says he is our great high priest who is interceding on our behalf. So this temple is God's command centre of all operations and Angels are being sent to earth to execute judgement against Satan's armies and all of his followers on earth. Angels are also being sent to the heirs of salvation, enabling them to do exploits as they did in the book of Daniel. It is God who is ruling Heaven and earth at all times, and these Angels are sent from his temple to smite all who are against him with these plagues.

HEAVENLY ANGELS ARE ENTRUSTED WITH MORE RESPONSIBILITY FOR GREATER FAITHFULNESS

Verse 7 "ONE OF THE FOUR LIVING CREATURES, GAVE THE SEVEN ANGEL'S, SEVEN GOLDEN VIALS, FULL OF THE WRATH OF GOD, WHO LIVES FOR EVER AND EVER."

All the future is in God's hands and all that happens on earth is sanctioned from the throne of God within the temple, as so many mighty Angels are participating in various ministries in Satan's three and a half year rule. They seem to be operating in various ranks, like in the army, with, Generals, captains, officers etc. and these Angels were presented with bowls (Vials) from one of the four creatures surrounding Gods throne.

If you remember in the seven seals, these cherubim's all assisted God, and here, at the end of the Devil's reign they are assisting in providing the plagues which end's with the final battle of Armageddon, So everything happening in the earth has been recorded for His Saints so they may understand, perfectly.

REVELATION CHAPTER 15 VERSE 8

THE TEMPLE IS CLOSED IN HEAVEN UNTIL ALL IS FULFILLED IN GOD'S PROPHETIC WORD.

Verse 8 "THE TEMPLE IN HEAVEN WAS FILLED WITH SMOKE, FROM THE GLORY OF GOD AND FROM HIS POWER, AND NO ONE COULD ENTER HIS TEMPLE, UNTIL THE SEVEN PLAGUES, OF THE SEVEN ANGELS WERE ENDED."

If we look at various Temples and the tabernacle in the Old Testament of the Bible, such as the one in the wilderness, God came down with his glory and no one could enter, until his glory was lifted. The same thing happened at the opening of Solomon's Temple when it was completed, the Glory of God came down and filled it, so here this Temple has been prepared for the arrival of the saints in the Resurrection. This re-opening of the Temple also comes after the Battle of Armageddon. "The last Battle" This is the time of the seventh Trumpet (Revelation Chapter10 verse 7) "but in that day of the trumpet sounded by the 7th.Angel, the mystery of God as he announced to his servants, the prophets, should be fulfilled".

All of the prophesies written of our Lord's second coming throughout the scriptures, will be fulfilled. Again, in Revelation Chapter.11 verse.15 when the kingdom of this world becomes the Kingdom of our Lord Jesus Christ, it says that when the 7th. Trumpet sounds the "Nations raged, but their wrath hath come" It goes on to say he will reward his servants the prophets, and saints and he will destroy those who are destroying the earth. This is the army which finally came to Armageddon and our Lord destroys them by the brightness of his coming.

In Revelation Chapter 11 verse19, it states the Temple in Heaven will be re-opened, at the same time, which we see was sealed before the last plagues. The last plague comes at the same time as the last trumpet, at the coming of our Lord, when they all appear before his throne, as in the seventh seal (Revelation Chapter 7 verses 9-14) "These are they who have just come out of the Great Tribulation", so all scripture of end times fits together so perfectly that if an uneducated man like myself can find the truth of it, so can you, with a little study, and the help of our amazing God.

REVELATION CHAPTER 16 VERSES 1 - 2

OUR GOD IS LORD AND COMMANDER OF ALL OPERATIONS

Verse 1 "THEN I HEARD A LOUD VOICE FROM THE TEMPLE, TELLING THE SEVEN ANGELS, "GO AND POUR OUT ON THE EARTH THE SEVEN BOWLS OF THE WRATH OF GOD."

The final command coming from within the temple, so we must assume it is God who is judging those who have accepted the devil to reign over them, Our God reigns in the heavens and also on the earth, and these seven plagues are poured out, on the devil's kingdom.

GOD'S WRATH AFFECTS ALL WHO WORSHIPPED THE DEVIL.

Verse 2 "SO THE FIRST ANGEL WENT AND POURED HIS BOWL ON THE EARTH AND FOUL, EVIL SORES CAME UPON MEN WHO BORE THE MARK OF THE BEAST AND WHO WORSHIPPED HIS IMAGE."

Notice who is giving this command, and who are the one's being judged. This judgment comes upon all the world from the four corners of the world, every individual person who has accepted the devil's mark, and worshipped his image, when Satan was ruling in the temple at Jerusalem, when he was sitting in the temple of God showing himself as God. (2 Thessalonians Chapter 2 verses.3 v.4)

So God is pouring these plagues out, upon every person who gives their allegiance to the devil, they must realise their judgment is coming from a righteous God, who is also a jealous God, and has given his Son, to save them, even His beloved Son, without any acceptance on the part of the inhabitants of the world, so it leaves him with no alternative, but to judge them in this way.

REVELATION CHAPTER 16 VERSES 3 - 7

GOD CONTROLS ALL THE LAWS OF HIS CREATION

Verse 3 "THE SECOND ANGEL POURED HIS BOWL INTO THE SEA, AND IT BECAME LIKE THE BLOOD OF A DEAD MAN, AND EVERY LIVING THING DIED THAT WAS IN THE SEA."

The earth is the Lord's and the fullness thereof, and at any time he is able to bring a judgment on his creation. I believe this may be worldwide or around the middle-east as the devil killed Gods two servants in Jerusalem and brings a world army against it in the last plague. Every-thing dies as the sea congeals like the blood of a dead man. So no life survives in it, it will end up like the Dead Sea, in the Middle-east.

GOD'S NEXT PLAGUE CONTAMINATES THE WORLD'S WATER SYSTEM

Verse 4 "THE THIRD ANGEL POURED HIS BOWL INTO THE RIVERS, AND THE FOUNTAINS OF WATER, AND THEY BECAME BLOOD, (**v5**) AND I HEARD THE ANGEL OF WATER SAY, "JUST, ART THOU, IN THY JUDGEMENTS. THOU, WHO ART, AND WAS, O HOLY ONE," (**v6**) "FOR MEN HAVE SHED THE BLOOD OF SAINTS AND PROPHETS AND THOU HAST GIVEN THEM BLOOD TO DRINK, IT IS THEIR DUE." (**v7**) AND I HEARD THE ALTAR CRY, "YEA LORD GOD THE ALMIGHTY, TRUE AND JUST ARE THY JUDGEMENTS."

Here God is passing judgement on the people of the earth, changing the water by turning it into blood showing He is our Creator. There is a reason for God's judgement as it is sanctioned from heaven. God is just in all his ways and all his judgements. The reason that they drink blood is because Christians have been killed world wide for their faith, There was a starting place called Jerusalem which is also referred to as Egypt and Sodom, where our

Lord was crucified, as we examine the next chapter, we see it called Babylon. The world was partaker of her sins, the killing of the saints of God.

Our God is a Holy God and a just God, in all his works, so our Lord has given them blood to drink for shedding the blood of his innocent Saints, and those in his temple in heaven agree with this judgement. Matthew, Chapter 23 verses 34 to 39, shows how in the city of Jerusalem, many prophets and saints died before Christ was crucified, then his Apostle's, Prophets, and Saints died. This sin has spread throughout the world, and it is estimated that 250,000. Christians are being killed every year.

REVELATION CHAPTER 16 VERSES 8 - 9

OUR LORD USES THE SUN AS A JUDGEMENT

Verse 8 "THE FOURTH ANGEL, POURED OUT HIS BOWL ON THE SUN AND IT WAS ALLOWED TO SCORCH MEN WITH FIRE."

Verse 9 "MEN WERE SCORCHED BY FIERCE HEAT, AND THEY CURSED THE NAME OF GOD, WHO HAD POWER OVER THESE PLAGUES, AND THEY DID NOT REPENT AND GIVE HIM GLORY."

God, created the sun in Genesis 1, for the benefit of the whole world. So there would be four seasons, a sowing season, a growing season a reaping season, and a resting season, also through the sun, we have a one year time system, and through the moon a twenty four hour day system. It's Gods wonderful time system that benefits the earth.

So here, we have God moving the sun, or using its heat to scorch Satan's worshippers in the earth, God uses the sun's rays for the purpose of bringing men to repentance, but the ungodly curse their Creator, and cry out in rage at the God who is bringing these plagues upon them.

Our God is very merciful, longsuffering and forbearing, willing that none should perish, but that all should come to repentance. But man is so hard-hearted against the Lord that nothing is able to turn him from his evil ways, this leaves God, no alternative, but to place him in hell for eternity, along with the millions and billions who worship the Beast in the great tribulation.

REVELATION CHAPTER 16 VERSES 10 - 11

GOD AFFLICTS SATAN'S THRONE IN JERUSALEM AT THE END TIMES

Verse 10 "THE FIFTH ANGEL, POURED HIS BOWL ON THE THRONE OF THE BEAST, AND ITS KINGDOM WAS IN DARKNESS, MEN GNAWED THEIR TONGUES IN ANGUISH,"

Verse 11 "AND CURSED THE GOD OF HEAVEN, FOR THEIR PAIN AND SORES, AND DID NOT REPENT OF THEIR DEEDS."

Our Lord is bringing many plagues upon the beast and his Kingdom; it is His last effort to bring transgressors to their senses, from Jerusalem to the ends of the world God brings these plagues of judgment upon the Kingdom of the beast.

Remember in Chapter 9, the Beast kills a third of the population of the world, and I believe this can only be achieved by long range missiles, with nuclear warheads. God may use these explosions by plunging the world into darkness or do it supernaturally.

The whole purpose of God in these plagues is to show he is still ruling in the world and everything in it being fulfilled according to his prophetic word. But men are so hardened in their hearts and blinded showing that Satan has totally deceived them and they are unable to turn from the deception of his evil ways.

So, the whole of Satan's Kingdom is suffering, and from their tongues come curses to the God of creation, who is pouring out these vials upon them, giving them the last chance to repent, and turn from the power of the beast and be saved.

REVELATION CHAPTER 16 VERSE 12

THE LAST SIGN OF THE FINAL BATTLE IN ISRAEL

Verse 12 "THE SIXTH ANGEL, POURED HIS BOWL ON THE GREAT RIVER EUPHRATES AND ITS WATER WAS DRIED UP TO PREPARE THE WAY FOR THE KINGS FROM THE EAST."

God controls all the seas and the rivers as in Moses day, he divided the Red Sea and so Israel could be delivered, and then closed it, on the Egyptian Army who had pursued them.

Again, when Joshua took Israel into the Promised Land, the Lord divided the river Jordan, so Israel could pass over on dry land, proving that our God controls all seas and rivers, and is able to change or interfere with his creation at any time as we have seen both in the Old and New testaments.

Here, he permits this great river Euphrates to be dried up, allowing a way for the Beast's mighty army from the east entry into Israel and Jerusalem as prophesied by his prophet in Ezekiel Chapters 39 and 40, and by other prophets in the Old testament and many more references to these events in the book of Revelation, Note also this army came from ten Eastern nations, who only could raise an army as large as this.

In Revelation chapter 9 Verses 14 -16 it gives us the number (200,000,000) and again, it spoke of the river Euphrates in the sixth trumpet, they are revealing the same incident as the sixth plague is described here, and so all the references of Revelation interlink.

REVELATION CHAPTER 16 VERSES 13 - 14

THE WORLD IS DECEIVED BY THE LYING WORDS OF THE DRAGON AND HIS ASSOCIATES

Verse 13 "AND I SAW ISSUING FROM THE MOUTH OF THE DRAGON AND FROM THE MOUTH OF THE BEAST AND FROM THE MOUTH OF THE FALSE PROPHET, THREE FOUL SPIRITS LIKE FROGS;"

Verse 14 "FOR THEY ARE DEMONIC SPIRITS PERFORMING SIGNS, WHO GO ABROAD TO THE KINGS OF THE WHOLE WORLD, TO ASSEMBLE THEM FOR BATTLE ON THE GREAT DAY OF GOD THE ALMIGHTY."

In chapter 13 we saw all members of the satanic trinity under the dragon's power. Here he imparts miracle power to the beast, and the false prophet to deceive the whole world, to make them believe they are representing the true God. Many people in the world have already been tricked into many deceptive religions, like black magic, spiritualism and many more national religions which have sprung up in the world, which are directly against the true faith, so that Kings and Kingdoms easily succumb to his powers of deception, to raise a world army to fight in Israel, against the true God Almighty.

In 2nd Corinthians Chapter 4 verse 4 it is written, he acts as the God of this world, who has blinded the minds of the unbelievers to keep them from seeing the light of the glory of Christ, who is the express image of God. But in the latter end of Satan's reign here, he deceives the Kings and Kingdoms to go to battle against Christ who is the Lord of Lords and the King of Kings.

In Revelation Chapter 14 Verse 19, speaking of the Lord's judgment it says " so the Angel swung his sickle on the earth and gathered the vintage of the earth and threw it into the great wine press of the wrath of God" so the vast army of Satan perished at the coming of the Lord.

REVELATION CHAPTER 16 VERSE 15

CHRIST IS COMING DIRECTLY AFTER THE LAST BATTLE IN ISRAEL

Verse 15 "LO I AM COMING LIKE A THIEF, BLESSED IS HE WHO IS AWAKE AND KEEPS HIS GARMENTS THAT HE MAY NOT GO NAKED AND BE SEEN EXPOSED"

Our Lord has promised us, he is coming a second time for all who look for him. Remember the ten virgins and how only the five wise virgins were ready for his coming, although the ten were looking for it. His coming is repeatedly told to us in the New Testament.

In the book of Revelation from chapter 4 to chapter 20 at the end of the seals, trumpets and the plagues is the coming of the Lord. How Bible expositors have not picked up on this truth, I will never know. The main instruction of this verse is the unexpectancy of the coming, and keeping our garments clean like the spotless Lamb of God, holy righteous and a garment of praise.

Christians should also know the signs of our Lords coming again, and should be ready to meet him. The danger is that Christians are neglecting the signs and are not themselves seeking to know for themselves this truth. At that time, iniquity will abound so that the love of many will grow cold, Matthew Chapter 24 v.10 "and then many will fall away and betray one another, and hate one another", v.11 "and many false prophets will arise and lead many astray", v.12 "and because wickedness is multiplied most men's love will grow cold" v.13 "but he that endures to the end shall be saved".

So keeping our garments is what this is speaking about, in these verses. Remember our Lord's parable of the man without a wedding garment who infiltrated into the banquet in heaven without a proper robe, and he was cast out. We are told no unclean person will enter into the presence of the Lord, so our aim is to be holy as our Lord is holy.

<u>**REVELATION CHAPTER 16 VERSES 16 - 18**</u>

<u>CHRIST'S JUDGEMENT FALLS ON SATAN'S ARMY, THEN ON THE WORLD.</u>

<u>**Verse 16**</u> "AND THEY ASSEMBLED THEM AT THE PLACE CALLED IN HEBREW, ARMAGEDDON. (**v17**) THE SEVENTH ANGEL POURED HIS BOWL INTO THE AIR, AND A LOUD VOICE CAME OUT OF THE TEMPLE FROM THE THRONE, SAYING "IT IS DONE". (**v18**) AND THERE WERE FLASHES OF LIGHTNING, VOICES, PEALS OF THUNDER, AND A GREAT EARTHQUAKE SUCH AS HAD NEVER BEEN SINCE MEN WERE ON THE EARTH, SO GREAT WAS THAT EARTHQUAKE."

<u>THE LAST BATTLE, THE LAST PLAGUE, THE LAST WORLD EARTHQUAKE, AT CHRIST'S COMING.</u>

The second coming of Christ to his Millennial reign happens when all that's been prophesied has been fulfilled, as it says in Revelation Chapter 10 verse 7. "But in the days of the trumpet call to be sounded by the 7th.trumpet, the mystery of God, as he announced to his servant the Prophet, should be fulfilled." Then in Chapter 11 verse 15, it says "Then the 7th. Angel blew his trumpet, and there were loud voices in heaven saying, the kingdom of the world has become the Kingdom of the Lord, and of his Christ, and he shall reign for ever and ever".

Again, talking of the beast and his army, in Chapter 17 verse 5, coming against Babylon the Great, the mother of harlots, and of earths abomination "and I saw a woman drunk with the blood of Martyrs of Jesus". Then go to verse 15, "the waters that you saw where the harlot is seated, are people, and multitudes, and nations" in verse 16, "the ten horns you saw, they and the Beast will hate the harlot, they will make her desolate and naked and devour her flesh, and burn her with fire".

In verse 17, "God has put it into their hearts, to carry out his purpose, by being of one mind and giving over their royal power to the Beast, until the Word of God is fulfilled. The woman is the great city which will have dominion over the kings of earth". So every prophesy concerning the second coming of Christ is fulfilled in Christ's Revelation to John, and all fits together like a jig saw puzzle, fitting together as a picture of the End time, unfolded before them in his word.

REVELATION CHAPTER 16 VERSES 19 - 21

THE DAY OF GOD'S JUDGEMENT FALLS ON THE ENTIRE WORLD.

Verse 19 "THE GREAT CITY WAS SPLIT INTO THREE PARTS, AND THE CITIES OF THE NATIONS FELL, AND GOD REMEMBERED GREAT BABYLON, TO MAKE HER DRAIN THE CUP OF THE FURY OF HIS WRATH."

Verse 20 "AND EVERY ISLAND FLED AWAY AND NO MOUNTAINS WERE TO BE FOUND."

Verse 21 "AND GREAT HAILSTONES, AS HEAVY AS A HUNDREDWEIGHT, DROPPED ON MEN FROM HEAVEN, UNTIL MEN CURSED GOD FOR THE PLAGUE OF THE HAIL, SO FEARFUL WAS THAT PLAGUE."

God is not only judging every ungodly person, he is also changing the whole structure of the world, as cities are destroyed, islands and every mountain disappear. God is destroying the whole face of the world, and the ungodly with their last breath curse God.

If only they would cry out in true repentance, as it is written, unless a man repent he cannot be saved and whosoever shall call on the name of the Lord shall be saved. It says, God is not willing that any should perish, but all should come to repentance.

Think of the millions passing into eternity daily at this time, and only a cry away from being saved. These sinful people are just like Pharaoh in Egypt, God gave him every chance to believe God and let Israel go but he hardened his heart so that it left God no alternative but to put him, and his army, away for eternity.

So our Lord is starting anew in his millennial reign, with the destruction of this city Jerusalem, then the cities of the world, all the ungodly people of the world, and for the saints of God, the Resurrection takes place on that same day, and they will ever be with the Lord.

REVELATION CHAPTER 17 VERSES 1- 3

Introduction

This chapter is a vital key in understanding the judgement of the Great City Babylon, also referred to as the Mother of Harlots and the earth's abomination, which will be destroyed on the last day, the day of the Lord's second coming. Remember in the previous chapter, this Angel came out of God's temple in heaven, to pour a vial on the seat of the kingdom of Satan, the Beast, the False Prophet, and on all who worship him. Satan has authority in the temple in Jerusalem, showing himself as God.

God is revealing this mystery prior to Christ's second coming through this Angel, so that his saints can follow each stage in detail, then they will have a perfect understanding of what is happening on the earth, and the reason for this final judgement. To fully understand this mystery, we will consider it, under the following heading and sub-headings.

THE MYSTERY OF BABYLON THE GREAT MOTHER OF HARLOTS

Verse 1 "ONE OF THE SEVEN ANGELS WHO HAD THE SEVEN BOWLS CAME AND SAID TO ME "COME, I WILL SHOW YOU THE JUDGEMENT OF THE GREAT HARLOT, WHO IS SEATED ON MANY WATERS".

All revelations concerning dreams, visions and mysteries in the Bible come from Gods throne, by the following ways, Angels being sent, or the Spirit of the Lord coming upon an Apostle, Prophet or Holy Person, giving understanding in a mystery. This Angel was on a mission, revealing the judgement of this great city Babylon, for her sins of the past; sins she has transmitted to the nations of the World. John had witnessed many events on earth in those last three and a half years, and is finally seeing the end, at Christ's coming. As we have just read of Satan's Judgement along with the Beast, in the previous chapter at the battle of Armageddon.

HOW THE HARLOT'S SINS, HAVE AFFECTED THE NATIONS OF THE WORLD.

Verse 2 "WITH WHOM THE KINGS OF EARTH HAVE COMMITTED FORNICATION, AND WITH THE WINE OF WHOSE FORNICATION, THE DWELLERS ON EARTH HAVE BECOME DRUNK."

John the Apostle, was a chosen vessel to reveal mysteries of all that Jesus had purposed him to write, concerning the last three and a half years, called "The Great Tribulation", and here, he is talking of the great city Babylon. This city has been a mystery to many expositors. Some of the evidence I will put forward, is when Satan is cast out of heaven. We find him in the temple in Jerusalem, showing himself as God. It was in this city, that Satan killed God's two servants, who also ministered for three and a half years; Revelation Chapter 11 v. 8 Jerusalem was that Great City which is spoken of here as Sodom and Egypt, where the Lord was crucified, look into these verses, in Zechariah, Chapter 14, verses 2 - 4. "For I will gather all nations against Jerusalem to battle, and the city shall be taken and the houses plundered, the women ravished, half of the city shall go into exile, but the rest of the people shall not be cut off from the city. Then the Lord will go forth and fight against those nations as when he fought on the day of battle. On that day his feet shall stand on the Mount of Olives, which lies before Jerusalem on the east, the Mount of Olives shall be split in two from east to west, by a very wide valley, so that one half of the Mount shall withdraw northward, and the other half southward.

You cannot deny that Christ's feet will touch the Mount of Olives, so why not believe the rest of the verses in context written here on Jerusalem. The Kings of the world have partaken with Jerusalem, in the sins of killing Prophets, Apostles and Saints. Even today, 250,000 Christians in the world, are dying as their Lord did. So the world has drunk from the same cup of wine of her fornication, until drunk with her sins, killing in the same way as the Anti-Christ did in Jerusalem.

GOD'S SERVANTS MOVE US INTO A HIGHER LEVEL OF UNDERSTANDING.

Verse 3 "AND HE CARRIED ME AWAY IN THE SPIRIT, INTO A WILDERNESS, AND I SAW A WOMAN SITTING ON A SCARLET BEAST, WHICH WAS FULL OF BLASPHEMOUS NAMES, AND IT HAD SEVEN HEADS AND TEN HORNS."

Holy men of God were moved by the spirit of God, in writing the Bible. Also men of God had dreams and visions from the Lord, and were moved to seek God, to give us understanding in these revelations that God was showing them. God is showing John the Apostle, a deeper understanding of the Beast, and the woman who is carried along by him. We will recapitulate some of his blasphemous names already mentioned, in Revelation Ch. 6 v.8, he speaks of the fourth rider as being called death, and hell followed him, who is Satan, in Ch. 9 v.11, he is called Angel of the bottomless pit, who is king of an international army, and also referred to him in Hebrew and Greek as Abaddon and Apollyon , also in Ch.12 v.9, we see other names such as the Great Dragon, ancient serpent, also called the Devil and Satan, the deceiver of the whole world.

Then in Revelation Ch.13 v.1- 2, it tells us of the Dragon's links with his two associates on earth the Beast who had already gained authority on the earth, to arrange a seven year peace agreement, along with the false prophet, for the coming of the Dragon. Ch.12 v.3 also shows that the Dragon has 7 heads, 10 horns, and 7 diadems, upon his heads, so the Beast prepared these nations for the Devil, when he was cast out of Heaven.

REVELATION CHAPTER 17 VERSES 4 - 6

THE HARLOT BABYLON DRESSED LIKE A QUEEN DISGUISES HER TRUE CHARACTER.

Verse 4 "THE WOMAN WAS ARRAYED IN PURPLE AND SCARLET AND BEDECKED WITH GOLD AND JEWELS AND PEARLS HOLDING IN HER HAND A GOLDEN CUP FULL OF ABOMINATIONS AND IMPURITIES OF HER FORNICATION."

Verse 5 "AND ON HER FOREHEAD WAS WRITTEN, A NAME OF MYSTERY "BABYLON THE GREAT, MOTHER OF HARLOTS AND EARTH'S ABOMINATIONS."

Verse 6 "AND I SAW THE WOMAN DRUNK WITH THE BLOOD OF THE SAINTS AND THE BLOOD OF THE MARTYRS OF JESUS."

This city of Jerusalem has transgressed the commandments of God, and killed his prophets in many generations both in the Old Testament as well as the New. Our Lord referred to this in Matthew Chapter 23 verses 34-35, "Therefore I send you prophets and wise men, scribes some of whom you will kill and crucify, and some you will scourge in your synagogues and persecute from town to town, that upon you may come all the righteous blood shed on the earth, from the blood of the innocent Abel, to the blood of Zechariah the son of Berechiah whom you murdered between the sanctuary and the altar, truly I say to you all, this will come upon this generation".

After this, they crucified Christ God's only begotten son then killed his apostles and prophets as well as his saints. The whole world followed in Jerusalem's sins, as the mother of harlots of the earth's abomination. She is described as being drunk with the blood of martyrs of Jesus.

At present, Israel is flourishing with prosperity, a few years ago, I made a visit to Israel, and was surprised when a courier said it was second only to America in the export of Computers and High-Tec. Components, so they could become a richer country financially in the end times.

REVELATION CHAPTER 17 VERSES 7- 8

THE MYSTERY REVEALED. THE WOMAN, 'THE BEAST' WITH SEVEN HEADS AND TEN HORNS.

Verse 7 "WHEN I SAW HER, I MARVELLED GREATLY BUT THE ANGEL SAID TO ME, "WHY MARVEL? I WILL TELL YOU THE MYSTERY OF THE WOMAN AND THE BEAST, WITH SEVEN HEADS AND TEN HORNS THAT CARRIED HER."

Our risen and glorified Lord is revealing in detail through his Angel to John, so that his church may understand who and what is written which has baffled many expositors for centuries, so it is of the utmost importance we listen and understand who the woman is, who the beast is with the seven heads and the ten horns, These all arise in the great tribulation with the dragon, who seeks world domination until all is fulfilled, that is prophetically spoken.

THE RISE AND FALL OF THE BEAST, SO CHRISTIANS MAY UNDERSTAND.

Verse 8 "THE BEAST THAT YOU SAW, WAS AND IS NOT, AND IS, TO ASCEND FROM THE BOTTOMLESS PIT AND GO INTO PERDITION. THE DWELLERS OF THE EARTH WHOSE NAMES HAVE NOT BEEN WRITTEN IN THE BOOK OF LIFE, FROM THE FOUNDATION OF THE WORLD, WILL MARVEL TO BEHOLD THE BEAST, BECAUSE IT WAS AND IS NOT, AND IS TO COME."

If we go back to Revelation Chapter 9 v.11 we see the beast of the bottomless pit and he is King, ruling over this international army that destroys a third of the population of the world, which is described in Verse 18. The beast continues from Chapter 9, to Chapter 17, and in other chapters it describes his activities in different ways. The Beast here goes into perdition. If we read 2 Thessalonians Chapter 2, verses 3-4 "Let no-one deceive you in any way, for that day will not come unless the rebellion comes first and the man of lawlessness is revealed the son of perdition, who opposes and exalts himself against every so called god or object of worship, so that he takes his seat in the temple of God, proclaiming himself as God". We accept this as the Anti-Christ upon the earth in the last days.

Turning back to Revelation Chapter 11 v.7 an Angel talks of Gods two servants who are using supernatural power in Jerusalem against the dragon, the Beast of the Bottomless pit, and the false prophet Verse 7 "When they had finished their testimony, the Beast that ascends from the bottomless pit will make war with them and kill them." In Verse 8 he then describes the place as Jerusalem, where our Lord was crucified. All the prophecies interlink with what our Glorified Lord is showing throughout Revelation.

Since many Christians have been influenced by books written by past expositors, they all have been led in various directions and doctrines. Be honest, how many hours have you personally studied this book? Remember I was led to study by the Lord, to spend 30 years as the Lord led me, after coming out of the Bible College, so I have given a little consideration to these studies. Christian brethren have believed many teachers' interpretations, but have never studied for themselves. I am amazed that the pre-Tribulation Rapture theory has been accepted and has been illustrated in the Schofield Bible as truth, so that it has spread and is believed by millions throughout the World.

One of England's most educated Preachers and expositors David Pawson, in one of his books revealed how this false doctrine, arose in England and how it was accepted by a Bible Publisher in America and spread throughout the world. I only hope and pray you will study Revelation with me to find the truth, as we are living in the last days and it is of the utmost importance that we come to the knowledge of the truth, so that we are prepared to pass through the great tribulation. I personally believe that our names are written before the foundation of the world,(in the lambs book of life.) But our Lord accomplishes this on his cross, and this gospel must be preached, to all the world, then we must repent of our sins and "Have Faith in Christ".

As we all have a free will to reject him with the Eternal consequences, or to accept him, then our names will be written in the Lamb's book of life. Jesus the Lamb, was purposed to be slain from the foundation of the world. There are many foundation truths, seven in all, which are connected with our Salvation, which are; repentance from dead works, Faith towards God, Two baptisms, one in water, one in his Spirit, the laying on of hands, the resurrection of the Dead and the eternal judgment, these are essential doctrines of our Faith, which I spent about

five years studying over my fifty years of being saved which has laid a good foundation in my faith, if we love God with all our hearts, I am sure we will study them first, then move on to perfection. "Study, to show yourself approved of God, a workman, who may not be ashamed, rightly dividing the word of Truth".

REVELATION CHAPTER 17 VERSES 9 - 11

GOD'S WISDOM IS REQUIRED TO UNDERSTAND HIS MYSTERIES.

Verse 9 "THIS CALLS FOR A MIND WITH WISDOM; THE SEVEN HEADS, ARE SEVEN HILLS ON WHICH THE WOMAN IS SEATED;"

Verse 10 "THEY ARE ALSO SEVEN KINGS, FIVE OF WHOM HAVE FALLEN, ONE IS, THE OTHER HAS NOT YET COME, AND WHEN HE COMES HE MUST REMAIN A LITTLE WHILE,"

Verse 11 "AS FOR THE BEAST THAT WAS AND IS NOT, IT IS AN EIGHTH, BUT IT BELONGS TO THE SEVEN, AND IT GOES TO PERDITION."

In this Chapter, in verse.18, we see this city referred to as the great city. In Chapter 11 v. 8 Gods two witnesses died in Jerusalem, and it is here referred to as the great City, where our

Lord was crucified. Jerusalem is also built upon seven mountains, which also proves it to be this City. She is also accused of being drunk with the blood of the Martyrs of Jesus. The Kings and Kingdoms all over the world have shared in her impure passion, and have martyred hundreds of millions throughout history.

Then he deals with the Kings of this City. John was on the isle of Patmos, and was an old man and five Kings were dead, the sixth was still reigning, then he switches over Two Thousand years, to this period of time, in which a seventh King, comes to the throne in Jerusalem, who prepares the way for the Dragon who is cast out of Heaven, and takes up his place with the Beast, who becomes the Man of sin, the Son of Perdition. 2 Thessalonians Chapter 2, verse 3.

Going back to Chapter 12, Chapter 13, and Chapter 14, we see Satan's whole activity, after being cast out of Heaven, and all the ways in which he attacks, the Christians worldwide. Then in Revelations Chapter 14, how God will judge him, his associates, and his vast army, written in verses 17 to 20.

REVELATION CHAPTER 17 VERSES 12 - 13

TEN KINGDOMS JOIN THE BEAST AND THE DRAGON FOR WORLD CONQUEST.

Verse 12 "THE TEN HORNS THAT YOU SAW, ARE THE TEN KINGS WHO HAVE NOT YET RECEIVED ROYAL POWER, BUT THEY ARE TO RECEIVE AUTHORITY AS KINGS FOR ONE HOUR, TOGETHER WITH THE BEAST. (**v13**) THESE ARE OF ONE MIND, AND GIVE OVER THEIR POWER AND AUTHORITY, TO THE BEAST."

I would now like to take you back to read a corresponding scripture to these verses in Daniel, Chapter 7 verses 23-26. This vision refers to the end times which you will see as you read it. (**v23**) Thus he said "As for the fourth Beast, there shall be a fourth kingdom on the earth, which shall be different from all the kingdoms, and it shall devour the whole earth, and trample it down and breaks it to pieces. **(v24)** And the ten horns out of this kingdom are the ten Kings that shall arise, and another shall arise after them and he shall be diverse from the first and he shall subdue three kings. **(v25)** He shall speak words against the Most High and shall wear out the saints of the Most High, and shall think to change the times of the law; they shall be given into his hands for a time, two times, and half a time (three and a half years, 42 months) **(v26)** But the court shall sit in Judgment, and his dominion shall be taken away to be consumed and destroyed to the end."

Daniel was receiving a dream and vision of what his lord also was giving John over two and a half thousand years later, Our Lord was planning this end from the beginning, there are hundreds of these prophetic scriptures in the Old Testament which fit into the book of Revelation. I believe what Bible expositors have tried to do, is to link these up, so that they had the truth sorted out, before Christ was glorified and gave us these final Chapters, which are revealed in the book of Revelation, where it gives us a perfect understanding of the end times.

This is the reason, we have various opposing views, which have divided His church, I hope the study of this book verse by verse will prepare us for his coming. These ten Kingdoms arise at the same time or just before Satan is cast down from Heaven to Earth. This is arranged by the Beast as seen in Rev. Ch. 13. At the end of the seals, the end of the trumpets, at the end of Chapter 14, then at the end of the plagues, it all finishes with the judgment of Satan and his army, at the coming of our Lord for His Saints. It is repeated so many times, it seems unbelievable that his Saints have missed this divine truth of Christ's coming.

REVELATION CHAPTER 17 VERSE 14

THE BATTLE BETWEEN THE LAMB OF GOD, AND THE DEVIL.

Verse 14 "THEY WILL MAKE WAR ON THE LAMB, AND THE LAMB WILL CONQUER THEM, FOR HE IS LORD OF LORDS AND KING OF KINGS, AND THOSE WITH HIM ARE CALLED AND CHOSEN AND FAITHFUL."

The Lamb of God is creator of all the world. In John's Gospel it says "He was in the world and the world was made by Him" When John the Baptist saw Jesus coming towards him, the Spirit of the Lord spoke out of him declaring Him to be the Lamb of God who takes away the sin of the world. Here the Devil has raised a mighty army, but what he fails to realize is he is fighting against the Lamb of God, the Creator of the world, Lord of Lords and King of Kings, the Almighty One, who is also the Judge of the entire World, and that this judgment belongs to God. It says He will destroy them by the brightness of his coming.

Remember the Devil's army has just destroyed 2.2 billion people by fire, brimstone and smoke on the earth. Revelation Ch. 9 v. 8 reads "By these three plagues a third of mankind was killed by fire, smoke and brimstone" This is written of the Beast of the Bottomless Pit's inter-national army, which we have proved in our past writings to be the Devil's army. As proclaimed here, judgement belongs to our God, he is a just God and his judgements are just.

Let us read Zechariah Ch.14 v.12 "This shall be the plague with which the Lord will smite people that wage war against Jerusalem; their flesh shall rot while they are still on their feet, their eyes shall rot in their sockets, their tongue shall rot in their mouths". Ask yourself, how much blood will run from the Army of 200 million? It will run up to the bridle of a horse.

The resurrection will have just taken place, so the Lord comes with those who are called, chosen and faithful. Both Matthew and Mark state "and then he will send out the Angels and gather his elect from the four winds from the ends of the earth to the ends of Heaven" . I believe some of us will rule from heaven and some will rule on earth both will have eternal life, if we hold fast to our faith until the end. Remember the Devil is let loose after One thousand years of Christ's millennial rule, and he is still able to muster a mighty army across the world before his army is destroyed and he is cast into hell.

REVELATION CHAPTER 17 VERSE 15

THE HARLOT RIDES ON THE POPULATIONS OF THE WORLD.

Verse 15 "AND HE SAID TO ME, "THE WATERS, THAT YOU SAW, WHERE THE HARLOT IS SEATED, ARE PEOPLE AND MULTITUDES, NATIONS AND TONGUES."

So Jerusalem has influenced the whole world with her sins of fornication which the kings and their kingdoms have committed i.e. the same sins of killing and shedding the blood of Christian Martyrs all over the world especially at this time when the Devil is cast out of heaven and he threatens all Christians with death, if they don't bow down and worship him.

When Adam and Eve were tempted by Satan, it affected every offspring in the world with a weakness in the flesh to sin when tempted. We have all sinned and transgressed the law of Almighty God. We cannot sin, until we come to an age of understanding the law as Paul states in Romans Chapter 7 v.7-10, you would not tell a small child not to steal, commit adultery, or fornication, as Paul says (v.9) "Without the law sin was dead, but when the law came, sin revived and I died". Paul was born under the law, from birth, but only understood it, at the age of understanding.

This was taught in the Pentecostal Bible College in the early 1930's by C L Parker, and his books are still available. Every person has broken God's law, so like Adam, we all have sinned, everyone in the world even in the end times. They are responsible for killing, as all the nations will be killing Christians, but we have a great assurance as Paul said, to be absent from the body is to be present with the Lord. So we have no fear of death, as our Lord is waiting for us.

The people of the world have shared in the sins of Jerusalem, "the Harlot". They are still responsible for any sins they have committed and will come to an eternal judgement, As it is written "All that are in the graves shall hear the voice of our Lord, and come forth, those who have done good, to the resurrection of life, and those who have done evil, to the resurrection of judgement". If any person transgresses His law, they will come to this judgement unless they have repented.

REVELATION CHAPTER 17 VERSES 16 - 18

THE DRAGON'S WORLD ARMY, PARTLY DESTROYS JERUSALEM.

Verse 16 "AND THE TEN HORNS THAT YOU SAW, THEY AND THE BEAST WILL HATE THE HARLOT; THEY WILL MAKE HER DESOLATE AND NAKED AND DEVOUR HER FLESH AND BURN HER WITH FIRE. (**v17**) FOR GOD HAS PUT IT INTO THEIR HEARTS, TO CARRY OUT HIS PURPOSE BY BEING OF ONE MIND AND GIVING OVER THEIR ROYAL POWER TO THE BEAST, UNTIL THE WORDS OF GOD SHALL BE FULFILLED. (**v18**) AND THE WOMAN THAT YOU SAW, IS THE GREAT CITY, WHICH HAS DOMINION OVER THE KINGS OF THE EARTH."

If we go back into Zechariah Ch. 14 v.1-4 it reads, "Behold a day of the Lord is coming, when the spoil taken from you will be divided in the midst of you, for I will gather all the nations against Jerusalem, to battle and the city shall be taken, the houses plundered the woman ravished; half the city shall go into exile, but the rest of the people shall not be cut off from the city.

Then the Lord will go forth and fight against those nations, as he fights on the day of battle, that day, his feet shall stand on the Mount of Olives which lies before Jerusalem on the east." We have here the same picture as in verse 16, this army assembled by the Dragon, the Beast and the false prophet, who have gathered 10 nations from the eastern countries to fulfil what God has spoken through his prophets of old. They are really fulfilling what God has spoken, but God still holds them responsible for their sinful actions, just as Judas Iscariot fulfilled a prophecy in selling his Lord for 30 pieces of silver, but was responsible for his own actions.

Look at the Jewish nation, banished for killing the Lord at Calvary, and calling for his blood to be on their shoulders. They have suffered through out many nations especially in the last war in Germany when 6 million were killed, I will ask you a question? Could the Lord have saved them from death as he saved Israel in Babylon from the evil Haman, who planned to kill all Israelites in captivity, for the Lord did save them through Esther, Mordecai and Ahasuerus. But our Lords blood is still on the shoulders of Israel, plus the blood of the Apostles, Prophets and Saints and God's two servants in Jerusalem.

God has promised to rebuild a New Jerusalem in the1000 years reign, He then will build a New Jerusalem in heaven bringing it to a New Earth to last for eternity. This Woman (v.18) is the Great City. On her forehead is the name, "Mystery Babylon" (v.5) referred to as Jerusalem in (Ch.11, v 8) the last battle rages in and around this Great City, it must be Jerusalem.

REVELATION CHAPTER 18 VERSES 1 - 2

Introduction This chapter continues with the Judgment of Babylon, and shows how its destruction affects not only this Great City, but also causes a knock on effect, throughout the world. It also describes how everything in this city came to a halt.

GOD'S ANGEL DESCRIBES THE JUDGEMENT OF THE GREAT CITY, BABYLON.

Verse 1 “AFTER THIS I SAW ANOTHER ANGEL COMING DOWN FROM HEAVEN HAVING GREAT AUTHORITY AND THE EARTH WAS MADE BRIGHT WITH HIS SPLENDOUR. (**v2**) HE CALLED OUT WITH A MIGHTY VOICE, FALLEN, FALLEN IS BABYLON THE GREAT! IT HAS BECOME A DWELLING PLACE OF DEMONS, A HAUNT OF EVERY FOUL SPIRIT, AND A HAUNT OF EVERY FOUL AND HATEFUL BIRD.

One of the three angels spoken in chapter 14, had the same message as spoken here, "Fallen, fallen is Babylon the great, she who made all the nations drink the wine of her impure passion?" But this mighty Angel had great authority from God, and a greater insight into this great city's destruction, remember that the last chapter and the last few verses, show that the Dragon, Beast, and false prophet fulfilled Gods prophetic word, when they destroy Jerusalem.

This was also, the place of the crucifixion of our Lord; it is not only the residence of Satan (as in 2 Thessalonians) but this verse also shows, all his demons and foul Spirits dwell there as well. We wrote earlier of how a third of his Angels were cast out of heaven, (In Revelations Chapter.12, verse. 9.) and took up residence here in Jerusalem and reigned around the world.

The Nations of the world have shared in her impure passion; this is the reason for God's many plagues and judgments, which he will bring upon the world and all the ungodly who receive the mark of the beast, since God's judgments are worldwide. So the nations of the world are drunk with her sins. They are responsible for their indulgence in her sins. Her sins have affected the merchants, for they have grown rich with her covetousness and idolatry, and made many traders rich by importing and exporting goods to and from Israel.

REVELATION CHAPTER 18 VERSES 3 - 6

THIS ANGEL IS WARNING CHRISTIAN'S TO FLEE FROM JERUSALEM

Verse 3 "FOR ALL THE NATIONS, HAVE DRUNK THE WINE OF HER IMPURE PASSION, AND THE KINGS OF THE EARTH HAVE COMMITTED FORNICATION WITH HER AND THE MERCHANTS OF THE EARTH HAVE GROWN RICH, WITH HER WEALTH AND HER WANTONNESS. (**v4**) THEN I HEARD ANOTHER VOICE FROM HEAVEN, SAYING COME OUT OF HER MY PEOPLE, LEST YOU TAKE PART IN HER SINS, LEST YOU SHARE IN HER PLAGUES. (**v5**) FOR HER SINS ARE HEAPED HIGH AS HEAVEN AND GOD HAS REMEMBERED HER INIQUITIES (**v6**) RENDER TO HER AS SHE HERSELF HAS RENDERED, AND REPAY HER DOUBLE FOR HER DEEDS, MIX A DOUBLE DRAUGHT FOR HER IN THE CUP SHE MIXED."

God is calling his people out of this city as they see the armies gathering at the river Euphrates. In Matthew Chapter 24 verse 16, it says "Let those who are in Judea, flee to the mountains", then in the same Chapter 24, verse 21, "For then there will be great tribulation". Again in Luke Chapter 21 verses 20-22, it says "But when you see Jerusalem surrounded by armies, then know that its desolation has come near, then let those who are in Judea flee to the mountains and let those who are inside the city depart, and let those who are out in the country not enter, for these are the days of vengeance to fulfil all that is written".

The people of Israel and Jerusalem had transgressed God's Law, throughout both the Old and New Testaments, and certain of their sins have spread all over the world. Like Sodom's sins had reached up to heaven and God judged them that they perished. Yet God gave Israel many blessings through Abraham, Isaac, Jacob and Moses, and all of the prophets, and when God sent his Son, they killed the Son of God.

Our Lord spoke a parable of Jerusalem as God's vineyard, and how he sent many prophets and they treated them badly, then at last he sent his only Son, and they killed him. Then he spoke of Judgement. Here she is paid double for all her sins and is judged by God. My prayer is for Israel, that these signs may turn many to the Christian faith, and the faith of those who have prayed for them so much, and for so long.

REVELATION CHAPTER 18 VERSES 7- 8

THE PRIDE OF HER OWN GLORY BROUGHT HER DESTRUCTION

Verse 7 “AND SHE GLORIFIED HERSELF AND PLAYED THE WANTON, SO GIVE HER A LIKE MEASURE OF TORMENT AND MOURNING, SINCE IN HER HEART SHE SAYS, " A QUEEN I SIT, I AM NO WIDOW, MOURNING I SHALL NEVER SEE". (**v8**) SO SHALL HER PLAGUES COME IN A SINGLE DAY, PESTILENCE AND MOURNING AND FAMINE, AND SHE SHALL BE BURNED WITH FIRE; FOR MIGHTY IS THE LORD GOD, WHO JUDGES HER.”

Once a person, a city or a nation, falls into pride, she falls into the trap of Satan. For he was lifted up with pride, when he desired to be like God in heaven. This was the temptation with which he attacked Adam and Eve, saying "Ye shall be like gods when you eat of the tree of knowledge". So this city, sits like a Queen, this was the cry of the false prophets, when the Babylonian armies stood outside the city, and Jeremiah a true prophet told the people they would go into captivity for seventy years. God, by the mouth of Jeremiah promised deliverance after seventy years in captivity. He then sent the Angel Gabriel to Daniel, with three more prophecies, (as found in Daniel Ch. 9 v. 24 - 27), 70 weeks of years (70x7 = 490 years), are determined upon Israel. Remembering that Daniel had already been in captivity 21 years, when this first prophesy was told, so in 7 weeks of years, which is 49, they would return to build up Jerusalem. This was confirmed in the days of King Artaxerx'es in Nehemiah Chapter 2. When he gives permission to restore Jerusalem as God had declared, then the second prophesy comes after 62 weeks of years = 434, here he is talking of Messianic predictions; his birth, his ministry, his death, his resurrection and his ascension. The gospel of Jesus Christ who died for the sins of the world to ensure all who repent and believe on God's Son's atoning blood for their sins are saved. These two prophesies cover 49 years + 434 = 483 years, then a third Prophesy comes after an indefinite period when there is a seven year peace agreement in the Middle East, as Nations seek a one world government. Then after three and a half years Satan is cast out of Heaven and the great tribulation breaks out, and all of our Lord's predictions spoken of in Rev.Ch.4 to 20, are fulfilled along with the abomination of desolation, then finally at the last battle, Armageddon, Babylon the great city is destroyed. 'Mighty is the Lord who judges her'. In the last Ch.17 v.16 'God shall put it into their hearts to carry out his purposes'. Remember God allowed his son to be killed in this city and they called for his blood to be upon them. I believe this is the reason they have suffered so much, also, God's two servants who were sent to stand against Satan, God allowed them to be killed in Jerusalem, then he resurrects them before the eyes of the world, This is why it continually says "Fallen, fallen is Babylon that great city, for Mighty is the Lord, that judges her".

REVELATION CHAPTER 18 VERSES 9 - 10

THE WORLD LAMENTS OVER THE FALL OF BABYLON.

Verse 9 "THE KINGS OF THE EARTH, WHO COMMIT FORNICATION AND WERE WANTON WITH HER, WILL WEEP AND WAIL OVER HER, WHEN THEY SEE THE SMOKE OF HER BURNING;"

Verse 10 "THEY WILL STAND FAR OFF, IN FEAR OF HER TORMENT, AND SAY, "ALAS, ALAS, THOU GREAT CITY, THOU MIGHTY CITY BABYLON! IN ONE HOUR HAS THY JUDGMENT COME."

The Kings of the earth have indulged in the same sins as Jerusalem, they have forsaken the God of Israel, and they have shed the blood of Christians, and have sought the riches and pleasures of the world.

This city, also called Babylon, was even spoken of in the Old Testament book of Isaiah Chapter 21 verse 9, it talks of her destruction "Fallen, Fallen is Babylon and all the images of her gods, He has shattered to the ground".

The battle of Armageddon is just a short distance from Jerusalem, and a vast army like this can annihilate a city like this within one hour. This city has been the centre of world attention since the Lord prophesied they would become a nation again.

This has stirred the anger of many Arab nations that surround them, and other nations are joining the Arabs to crush them, but, the world and its armies will all fall under Gods judgement, as recorded in the scriptures.

REVELATION CHAPTER 18 VERSES 11 - 13

HOW THE RUIN OF THIS CITY, AFFECTS THE WORLD ECONOMY

Verse 11 "AND THE MERCHANTS OF THE EARTH WEEP AND MOURN FOR HER, SINCE NO ONE BUYS THEIR CARGO ANY MORE,"

Verse 12 "CARGOES OF GOLD, SILVER AND JEWELS AND PEARLS, FINE LINEN PURPLE SILK, AND SCARLET, ALL KINDS OF SCENTED WOOD, ALL ARTICLES OF IVORY, ALL ARTICLES OF COSTLY WOOD, BRONZE, IRON AND MARBLE,"

Verse 13 "CARGOES OF CINNAMON, SPICE, INCENSE, MYRRH, FRANKINCENSE, WINE OIL, FINE FLOUR AND WHEAT, CATTLE AND SHEEP, HORSES AND CHARIOTS AND SLAVES, THAT IS HUMAN SOULS."

This is the great city that was at the centre of biblical history which was destroyed at other times in history for desiring other gods and lusting after the sins of other nations. This city will be the centre of the world trade and the largest importer of goods in the world; she will probably be the richest city in the world at that time. This great city where Satan was found in the temple of God, showing himself as God ruling the world, Satan had prospered after extinguishing a third of the world's population along with a third of the vegetation of the world. So here he is ruling world trade and making many merchants of the sea, rich, from trade to and from Israel, especially Jerusalem.

The Lord told a parable of living for the riches of this life and leaving God out of our lives. This rich man grew richer and richer so he decided to build bigger and bigger barns, then he said, "I can sit and rest and have an early retirement" but God said "Thou fool, thy soul is required this night" This means Death would strike that very night, then his soul which is the eternal part of a man, will find itself in Hades. For it is written, who then can retain his spirit at death for it returns back to God, who gave it, his body returns to dust leaving his soul, either in heaven or in hell. So this great city perishes and vanishes like our bodies, and all her life stops so suddenly, and within one hour, when her enemy destroys her.

REVELATION CHAPTER 18 VERSES 14 - 19

GOD'S FINAL JUDGEMENT ON THE GREAT CITY AFFECTS ALL SOULS.

Verse 14 "THE FRUIT WHICH THY SOUL LONGED FOR, HAS GONE, AND ALL RICHES, AND THY SPLENDOUR ARE LOST TO THEE, NEVER TO BE FOUND AGAIN. (**v15**) THE MERCHANTS OF THESE WARES, WHO GAINED WEALTH FROM HER, WILL STAND FAR OFF, IN FEAR OF HER TORMENT, WEEPING AND MOURNING ALOUD (**v16**) "ALAS, ALAS, FOR THAT GREAT CITY, THAT WAS CLOTHED IN FINE LINEN, IN PURPLE AND IN SCARLET, BEDECKED WITH GOLD, WITH PRECIOUS JEWELS AND WITH PEARLS. (**v17**) IN ONE HOUR, ALL THIS GREAT WEALTH HAS BEEN LAID WASTE," EVERY SEA CAPTAIN AND THOSE WHO MADE THEIR LIVING, STOOD FAR OFF. (**v18**) AND CRIED OUT AS THEY SAW THE SMOKE OF HER BURNING. "WHAT CITY WAS LIKE THE GREAT CITY?" (**v19**) AND THEY THREW DUST ON THEIR HEADS, AS THEY WEEP AND MOURN CRYING OUT "ALAS, ALAS, FOR THE GREAT CITY, WHERE ALL WHO HAD SHIPS AT SEA, GREW RICH BY HER WEALTH! IN ONE HOUR SHE HAS BEEN LAID WASTE."

Babylon is this great city , this city is called by other names, such as Sodom and Egypt where our Lord was crucified, which identifies it as Jerusalem, It is Jerusalem where God's two servants came, Revelation Chapter 11 verse 7-8 and prophesied throughout Anti-Christ's reign before he killed them. No wonder this judgement is proclaimed so many times from Chapter 14 onwards, Fallen, Fallen is Babylon the Great, this city drunk with the blood of Saints and the blood of the martyrs of Jesus, Rev. 17 v. 5-6. In the last days when Satan rules the world this city becomes the greatest city in the world, for we read, that the merchants of the seas were made rich with her wares.

At the end of time, Jerusalem becomes one of the greatest cities in the world and the greatest importer and exporter of goods, when the world is going through an economic crisis with a third world war, disasters and plagues all coming on the earth together. At this time, ten Nations come against Israel, they gather at the river Euphrates, the four Angels were released who had held them at the river for an hour, a day, a month and a year, to destroy a third of all mankind. Then this mighty army came towards Jerusalem and passed over the river Euphrates. So our Lord has set a time for Jerusalem to fall, and all these events are to be fulfilled, then he will annihilate this army. The smoke from this city will be seen miles out to sea, by the traders of the seas, they will weep and wail as their employment ceases and all their future comes to an end. Then our Lord will destroy all the ungodly in the world before he starts his millennial reign.

REVELATION CHAPTER 18 VERSES 20 - 21

THE FALL OF JERUSALEM, BRINGS JOY IN HEAVEN.

Verse 20 "REJOICE OVER HER, O HEAVEN, SAINTS AND APOSTLES AND PROPHETS, FOR GOD HAS GIVEN JUDGMENT FOR YOU AGAINST HER."

Verse 21 "THEN A MIGHTY ANGEL TOOK UP A STONE LIKE A MILLSTONE THREW IT INTO THE SEA SAYING "SO SHALL BABYLON THE GREAT CITY BE THROWN DOWN WITH VIOLENCE AND SHALL BE FOUND NO MORE"."

Heaven is rejoicing because of all those saints who have been persecuted and killed for centuries in Jerusalem, that have been avenged. Matthew 23 v.34-35, 'therefore I send you prophets and wise men and scribes, some of whom you will kill and crucify, and some you will scourge in your synagogues and persecute from town to town, that upon you may come all the righteous blood shed on earth, from the blood of innocent Abel to the blood of Zechariah the son of Berechiah, whom you murdered between the sanctuary and the altar'.

The world has followed, in murdering Apostles prophets and saints of Jesus Christ, but all the saints of our Lord since his resurrection had a special place in Heaven. Rev. ch.6 v.9-10, I saw under the altar the souls of those slain for the Word of God and for the witness they had borne, they cried with a loud voice "O Sovereign Lord, Holy and true, how long before thou wilt judge and avenge our blood on those who dwell upon the earth".

So the world, like Jerusalem has carried on shedding the blood of Christians, that at this present time, it is quoted 250,000 are dying for their faith every year. Our Lord is coming to pour out his judgement upon the earth from Jerusalem to the ends of the world and collect his saints for Heaven, also those who reign upon the earth in his millennial reign. No wonder all heaven rejoices when all sin comes under Gods judgement.

REVELATION CHAPTER 18 VERSES 22 - 24

THE FALL OF THIS CITY CAUSES ALL SOUND, LIGHT, AND LIFE, TO CEASE IN IT.

Verse 22 "AND THE SOUND OF THE HARPERS AND MINSTRELS OF FLUTE PLAYERS AND TRUMPETERS, SHALL BE HEARD IN THEE NO MORE. AND A CRAFTSMAN OF ANY CRAFT SHALL BE FOUND IN THEE NO MORE, AND THE SOUND OF THE MILLSTONE SHALL BE HEARD IN THEE NO MORE."

Verse 23 "AND THE LIGHT OF A LAMP SHALL SHINE IN THEE NO MORE; AND THE VOICE OF BRIDEGROOM AND BRIDE SHALL BE HEARD IN THEE NO MORE; FOR THY MERCHANTS WERE THE GREAT MEN OF THE EARTH, AND ALL NATIONS WERE DECEIVED BY THY SORCERY."

Verse 24 "AND IN HER WAS FOUND THE BLOOD OF PROPHETS, AND OF SAINTS, AND ALL WHO HAVE BEEN SLAIN ON EARTH."

The fall of this city is similar to death in a person's life, everything in life disappears forever, and everything mentioned above is gone, lost forever, unless you have a personal relationship with God, through the death and resurrection of his beloved Son.

So Satan has ruled from this city and deceived the world to worship him. All craft and pleasures cease. What you are able to work with your hands, also all sports that they love to participate in, are all left behind. Then all employment such as textile factories, plastic factories, car factories and generators etc, are all destroyed.

No more marriages, or family re-unions no more coming together, when death or destruction comes, no wonder the Bible says "What does it profit a man if he gains the whole world and looses his soul". In this city, gathered all the rich merchants of the world around Satan, money is of no value when death strikes, covetousness is idolatry. This is one of the reasons for God's world judgment.

REVELATION CHAPTER 19 VERSES 1 – 3

Introduction We will divide this chapter, under the following headings;

1. THE GLORY AND JUDGEMENT AT CHRIST'S SECOND COMING
2. GOD LEAVES AN ETERNAL SIGN OF THIS JUDGEMENT
3. ALL HEAVEN EXPLODES IN WORSHIP AT THE LORDS SALVATION
4. THE HEAVENLY MARRIAGE OF CHRIST AND HIS BRIDE
5. THE DANGER OF VENERATING MINISTERS WITH REVELATION OF END TIMES
6. THE WORDS THAT DESCRIBE JESUS AS GOD'S SON AT HIS SECOND COMING
7. CHRIST'S CALL TO THE BIRDS TO FEAST ON THE CARCASSES AFTER ARMAGEDDON

THE GLORY AND JUDGEMENT AT CHRIST'S SECOND COMING

Verse 1 "AFTER THIS I HEARD WHAT SEEMED TO BE THE LOUD VOICE OF A GREAT MULTITUDE IN HEAVEN CRYING "HALLELUJAH SALVATION AND GLORY AND POWER BELONG TO OUR GOD"."

Verse 2 "FOR HIS JUDGEMENTS ARE TRUE AND JUST. HE HAS JUDGED THE GREAT HARLOT WHO CORRUPTED THE EARTH WITH HER FORNICATION; HE HAS AVENGED ON HER THE BLOOD OF HIS SERVANTS."

All heaven breaks out in praise and worship as the last judgment is administered on the earth. It seems that the whole of heaven glories in their God as they are crying out with loud voices, praising God. Look at what God is praised for; Salvation of man, complete deliverance from Satan and his power. Going back to Revelation Chapter.12 verse.10, "Now the salvation and the power and the kingdom of our God and the authority of his Christ have come, for the accuser of our brethren has been thrown out."

It is only when Satan is cast out of Heaven, that salvation comes to Heaven, and it is only when Satan is put away first for a thousand years, that we find our salvation comes to the earth; then we will join with the heavenly host in loud voices singing of our redemption and salvation. It is at this time, when the trumpet sounds and all the dead in Christ shall arise and be caught up to meet him in the air, for the judgement of God falls on Babylon the Great, this great city Jerusalem, Luke Ch.21 v.20, 'but when you see Jerusalem surrounded by armies then know that its desolation is near'. Verses 25-27 'and there will be signs in sun, moon and stars, and upon the earth, distress of nations and perplexity at the roaring of the sea, and the waves, men fainting with fear, and foreboding of what is coming on the world, for the powers of heaven will be shaken, and then they will see the Son of Man coming in the cloud with power and great glory'.

So our Lord comes at this time with Salvation, Glory, and great Power, also he comes to execute his final judgement, not only on the armies of Anti-Christ, who have just destroyed his city, Jerusalem, but also on Jerusalem, because Jerusalem has killed the Prophets, Saints and those who have believed in Christ right up to this day. They had killed Gods two Prophets, and are killing all who will not worship the Beast or accept his mark. Because the world has indulged in its sins of killing the saints of God, so they will come under his wrath in the last days. He must cleanse the world for the start of Christ's millennial reign.

GOD LEAVES AN ETERNAL SIGN OF THIS JUDGEMENT

Verse 3 "ONCE MORE THEY CRIED, HALLELUYAH! THE SMOKE FROM HER GOES UP FOR EVER AND EVER."

God leaves a sign which will last generation to generation until we run into a new start, a new beginning, in his eternal plan. This being the millennial reign of Christ. Whether he adds another sign to the rainbow which was a reminder of this last judgement after the flood, - a promise he would not flood the earth again. Is this smoke to rise as another eternal sign to this judgement as the beast and the false prophet are cast into hell where the worm does not die, nor is the fire quenched. - Eternal Punishment.

Satan is chained up for the thousand year reign of Christ, after that, he begins his old deception so God finally puts him in Hell forever. This smoke will act to show the mercy of God to all believers, who have put their faith in his beloved Son, Jesus Christ who has redeemed them from sin and the eternal fire of hell.

REVELATION CHAPTER 19 VERSES 4 – 6

ALL HEAVEN EXPLODES IN WORSHIP AT OUR LORD'S SALVATION

Verse 4 "AND THE TWENTYFOUR ELDERS, AND THE FOUR LIVING CREATURES, FELL DOWN AND WORSHIPPED GOD, WHO IS SEATED ON THE THRONE, SAYING "AMEN, HALLELUYAH". (**v5**) AND FROM THE THRONE CAME A VOICE CRYING "PRAISE OUR GOD ALL YOU HIS SERVANTS, YOU WHO FEAR HIM SMALL AND GREAT". (v6) THEN I HEARD, WHAT SEEMED TO BE A VOICE OF A GREAT MULTITUDE, LIKE THE SOUND OF MIGHTY THUNDERPEALS, CRYING "HALLELUJAH! FOR THE LORD OUR GOD REIGNS"."

The inhabitants of Heaven, every angel assembles for this great victory on earth, when God allowed this great city to be destroyed, by this army of Anti-Christ, for her sins have reached to the ends of the world. Then God throws his two associates, the Beast and the false Prophet into hell placing Satan, in the pit, in chains, for a thousand years, and removing the vast army and all who worshipped the Devil. Remember when judgment ceases the resurrection of Christians takes place, all who are in the graves will come out, those who have done good, to Eternal Life, for corruption must put on in-corruption and mortality must put on immortality when the last trumpet sounds, as spoken of in 1st Corinthians, Chapter 15 verses 51-53, also Revelation Chapter 11 verses 15-18, reveals that when the seventh and last trumpet sound, verse 18, 'the nations raged but thy wrath comes and the time for the dead to be judged, for the rewarding the prophets and Saints'.

Two events, written here, happen on the same day, judgment of the ungodly and the resurrection of his Saints. It is written, we all must give an account of our deeds done in the body, to whom much is given, much is required, we see this happening in the talents, given to saints, five, two, and one, and how they traded with these talents to bring more talents and are then rewarded for their labour, Matthew Chapter 25 verses 14-30.

It is very serious to neglect the gifts given to us. It is because of our inheritance at this time, all heaven joins in worshipping their God for redeeming the saints to heaven, and worship explodes throughout the whole of heaven. No one can imagine millions and millions of this magnitude singing, praising and worshipping God, as He fulfils his promise as spoken in His prayer, that He taught the disciples "thy will be done on earth as in heaven". So let us look up, for the redemption draws near, the redemption of our bodies. It is then that the earth becomes Christ's footstool.

REVELATION CHAPTER 19 VERSES 7- 9

THE HEAVENLY MARRIAGE OF CHRIST, AND HIS BRIDE.

Verse 7 “LET US REJOICE AND EXALT AND GIVE HIM THE GLORY, FOR THE MARRIAGE OF THE LAMB HAS COME, AND HIS BRIDE HAS MADE HERSELF READY,”

Verse 8 “IT WAS GRANTED HER TO BE CLOTHED WITH LINEN, BRIGHT AND PURE, FOR THE FINE LINEN IS THE RIGHTEOUS DEEDS OF THE SAINTS,”

Verse 9 “AND THE ANGEL SAID TO ME, "WRITE THIS; BLESSED ARE THOSE WHO ARE INVITED TO THE MARRIAGE SUPPER OF THE LAMB" AND HE SAID TO ME, "THESE ARE THE TRUE WORDS OF GOD".”

This rejoicing in Heaven, brings a voice crying out from the throne, where the four cherubim and the twenty-four elders are. This voice from the throne encourages praise and worship, as the words are speaking of a heavenly marriage which has just taken place, when the sons of God are resurrected to Christ, for he has cleansed and betrothed them as his bride for heaven.

The garments presented to them, declared the righteous deeds we have done by our faith in our Lord Jesus Christ. What an inheritance we have waiting on our arrival in heaven, the whole of heaven singing and rejoicing for this special day. We are told there is rejoicing in heaven over one sinner that repents, three times he repeats this in the gospel, the lost coin, the lost sheep, and the lost son who repented, But here, we have the arrival of millions, of repented sinners, who have washed in the blood of the lamb and now are presented with robes fit for heaven.

Christians must be over-comers on earth like their Lord who was tempted at all points as we are, yet without sin. The trial of our faith is much more precious than gold that has been tried by fire. The Lord has waited over two thousand years for the resurrection of the Bride of Christ, and he meets them in the air, as he takes his Bride as his own, and she is presented with the heavenly robes, which she had gained by her deeds of faith.

REVELATION CHAPTER 19 VERSE 10

THE DANGER OF VENERATING MINISTERS WITH REVELATION OF END TIMES

Verse 10 "THEN I FELL DOWN AT HIS FEET TO WORSHIP HIM, BUT HE SAID TO ME "YOU MUST NOT DO THAT! I AM A FELLOW SERVANT WITH YOU AND YOUR BRETHREN, WHO HOLD THE TESTIMONY OF JESUS, WORSHIP GOD." FOR THE TESTIMONY OF JESUS IS THE SPIRIT OF PROPHESY."

If an apostle such as John can be carried away by an Angel's ministry in such a way, as to fall down and worship him, then there is a danger to all the Saints that a minister can draw a congregation by his ministry, to worship himself.

We must learn this lesson, not to look on Servants of God, as Lords, they are just brethren like ourselves, a true servant will correct this immediately, like this Angel, and show them the revelation they are revealing, belongs to God.

So we must all realise there is only one God, and him only, shall we worship. All ministry gifts such as Apostle, Prophet, Pastor-teachers, evangelist, are servants, not Lords, there is only one Lord, He who died for our sins, who rose again on the third day, according to His word, and He sits at his Fathers side, until the earth becomes His footstool.

He alone, Jesus, is Lord of our salvation, He is our redemption, and He alone is the one we worship. He has the words of 'Eternal Life', and the testimony of Jesus is the spirit of Prophecy.

REVELATION. CHAPTER 19 VERSES 11 - 16

THE WORDS THAT DESCRIBE JESUS AS GOD'S SON AT HIS COMING.

Verse 11 "THEN I SAW HEAVEN OPEN AND BEHOLD A WHITE HORSE! HE WHO SAT UPON IT IS CALLED FAITHFUL AND TRUE, AND IN RIGHTEOUSNESS HE JUDGES AND MAKES WAR. (**v12**) HIS EYES WERE LIKE FLAMES OF FIRE AND ON HIS HEAD ARE MANY DIADEMS AND HE HAS A NAME INSCRIBED WHICH NO ONE KNOWS BUT HIMSELF. (**v13**) HE IS CLAD IN A ROBE DIPPED IN BLOOD, AND THE NAME BY WHICH HE IS CALLED IS 'THE WORD OF GOD' (**v14**) AND THE ARMIES OF HEAVEN, ARRAYED IN FINE LINEN WHITE AND PURE, FOLLOWED HIM ON WHITE HORSES (**v15**) FROM HIS MOUTH ISSUED A SHARP SWORD WITH WHICH TO SMITE THE NATIONS, AND HE WILL RULE THEM WITH A ROD OF IRON; HE WILL TREAD THE WINE PRESS OF THE FURY OF THE WRATH OF GOD THE ALMIGHTY (**v16**) ON HIS ROBE AND ON HIS THIGH HE HAS A NAME INSCRIBED ' KING OF KINGS AND LORD OF LORDS'."

In these few verses we see the Son of God coming from heaven in glory. The Lord repeatedly spoke of his coming again to the earth, in John Chapter 14 verse 2, He says "In my fathers house are many rooms, I go to prepare a place for you," He then says " I will come again and take you to myself, that where I am you may be also" On another occasion in Acts Chapter 1 verse 10 after Jesus', ascension to heaven, two Angels appeared saying " Men of Galilee, why do you stand looking up to heaven? This same Jesus, who is taken from you, will come in the same way as you saw him go to heaven.

In Revelation Chapter 1 verse 7 it says 'Behold he is coming in the clouds and every eye shall see him, everyone who pierced him and all the tribes of the earth will wail on account of him.' Even so, come - "I am the Alpha and Omega" says the Lord God, who is and was and who is to come, so this is going to be a glorious return of our Lord, as it says in Thess.Ch.4 v.16 ' For the Lord himself will descend from heaven with a cry of command, with an archangel call and with the sound of the trumpet of God, and the dead in Christ will rise first, then we who are alive and who are left, will be caught up together with them in the clouds to meet the Lord in the air, and so we shall always be with the Lord.'

Then we see, coming back to verse 11 'And in righteousness he judges and makes war, God must judge the nations of the world who do evil. Then in Revelation Ch. 6 v 12, it says in the sixth seal, at Christ's coming, the sun, and moon are changed and the stars will fall from heaven to earth. Going forward to verse 16, these sinners are crying out, calling on the mountains and rocks "fall on us, and hide us from the face of Him who is seated on the throne, and from the wrath of the Lamb". Then verse 17, 'for the great day of their wrath has come, and who can stand before him'.

In Revelation chapter 7 verse 5 to 11, we see the resurrection saints before the throne of the Lamb in Heaven. Again coming forward to verse 14, it says of these saints who have just arrived in Heaven, John was informed by one of the Elders, who are before God, "These have just come out of great tribulation, they have washed their robes and made them white in the blood of the lamb. Therefore they are before the throne of God." In the seventh trumpet, speaking again of Christ's coming found in Revelation Chapter 11 verse 18, 'for the nations raged, but thy wrath came, and the time for the dead to be judged for rewarding thy servants the prophets and saints', then a couple of lines further on, he says he will destroy those who are destroying the earth.

Going back to when our Lord was speaking of the signs of his coming, in Matthew 24 verses 29-31, "Immediately after the tribulation of those days the sun will be darkened and the moon will not give her light and the stars will fall from heaven, and the powers of the heavens will be shaken." Then in verse 30, 'Then will appear the sign of the Son of Man in heaven, and then all the tribes of the earth will mourn and they will see the Son of Man coming on the clouds of Heaven with power and great glory', verse 31, 'and he will send out his angels with a loud trumpet call, and they will gather his elect from the four winds, from one end of heaven to the other'. Two events are seen in these scriptures, regarding Christ's second coming, one, of judgement on the ungodly and the other, the resurrection of his saints.

Coming back to the original verses in our text, in verse 12 it speaks of his eyes being like flame, keeping in mind our heading, that Jesus is God, in flesh, but know that he is glorified with the glory he had with his father before the world began, as equal in creation and the God head. In Revelation chapter 1 verse 14, it says, 'His eyes were like a flame of fire'. Here he is describing the Glorified Christ, on to verses 17 & 18 he says " I am the first and the Last, and the living one, I died, and behold I am alive for evermore, and I have the keys of death and Hades".

In the text verse 13 he is clad in robes dipped in blood and his name is the Word of God. The Bible says Christ was marred more than any man. Look at the affliction he had to bear like a crown of thorns, piercing his head, his back ploughed like a field as the whip lashed his back, buffeted and bruised until he was black and blue, then nails in his hands and feet all this he bore for our sins, to redeem us from our sins. What a wonderful God we have, who laid down his life suffering in this way. In this verse he also reveals himself as the Word of God.

In the gospel of John Ch.1 v 1-3 it says 'In the beginning was the Word, and the Word was with God, and the Word was God, all things were made through him and without him was not anything made that was made'. So we see equality in the Godhead between Father and Son, Jesus said "My Father and I are one, if you have seen me, you have seen the father". Then in John Ch. 1 v.14 we read ' and the Word (Jesus) became flesh and dwelt among us, full of grace and truth, and we beheld his glory, the glory of the only Son from the Father'. Jesus Christ is God's Son in the Godhead.

So the Word is from Christ's mouth! (Rev.19 v.15) When he comes he will smite the nations of the world. So he comes in judgment on all the ungodly, then he will tread the wine press of his fury of the wrath of God. Linking this with the sixth seal, Revelations Chapter 6 verses 16-17 it says, 'Hide us from him who is seated on the throne and from the wrath of the Lamb.' Then another scripture relating to Satan's judgement and his army, is found in Revelation Chapter 14 verses 19-20, 'So the Angel swung his sickle on the earth, and threw it into the great wine press of the wrath of God, and the wine press was trodden outside the city and blood flowed from the wine press, as high as a horse's bridle for one thousand six hundred stadia'.

So Jesus is Saviour of the world, and he is also Judge of all the World. This is the reason, in the last line of verse 16, it states written on our Lords thigh, is the name, "King of Kings and Lord of Lords". So He who created the world is Lord of the World and also He is King of all Kingdoms of the World. When He comes again, He will rule with a rod of iron against anyone who breaks his laws of love.

REVELATION CHAPTER 19 VERSES 17- 19

CHRIST CALLS THE BIRDS TO FEAST ON THE CARCASSES AFTER ARMAGEDDON

Verse 17 "THEN I SAW AN ANGEL STANDING IN THE SUN AND WITH A LOUD VOICE HE CALLED TO ALL THE BIRDS THAT FLY IN MID HEAVEN,"

Verse 18 "COME, GATHER FOR THE GREAT SUPPER OF GOD,"

Verse 19 "TO EAT THE FLESH OF KINGS THE FLESH OF CAPTAINS, THE FLESH OF MIGHTY MEN, THE FLESH OF HORSES AND THEIR RIDERS AND THE FLESH OF ALL MEN BOTH FREE AND SLAVE, BOTH SMALL AND GREAT."

Our Lord is the God of creation and all therein. Every bird is under his authority and he is able to call and gather them together for this feast. While on holiday in Israel I was told that millions of birds migrating from various countries pass over Israel, so that the air-force planes have to take off over the Mediterranean Sea to gain altitude to ascend above the birds. There is going to be 200,000,000 carcasses left to be eaten by the birds of the air that is mentioned in the verse above and in Matthew Chapter 24, v 28 and Ezekiel Chapter 39 v.4. In Revelation Chapter 17 v 13-14 talking of this mighty army gathered with the Beast, it says "these are of one mind and give over their power and authority to the beast they will make war on the Lamb, and the Lamb will conquer them, for he is Lord of Lords, and the King of Kings, and those with him are called and chosen and faithful". In the sixth seal, Chapter 6, verse 16, it says 'hide us from the wrath of the Lamb', also in Chapter 11 verse18, "The nations raged as thy wrath came".

Then at the end of Satan's reign, his army falls under God's judgment as it is poured out. It says in Revelation Chapter 14 verse 19, "He gathered the vintage of the earth, and threw it into the great wine press of the wrath of God", so at the end of the seals also the trumpets and the pouring out of Gods wrath, then the last plague ends with the last battle Armageddon. So all through the book of Revelation it is describing the same end times, the last 42 months of Satan's reign upon the earth, and all end with this judgment and the resurrection of His saints for heaven, and others to rule on earth.

REVELATION CHAPTER 19 VERSES 20 - 21

ETERNAL JUDGMENT FALLS IN VARIOUS WAYS AT THE END

Verse 20 "AND THE BEAST WAS CAPTURED AND WITH IT, THE FALSE PROPHET WHO IN ITS PRESENCE HAD WORKED THE SIGNS BY WHICH HE DECEIVED THOSE WHO HAD RECEIVED THE MARK OF THE BEAST AND THOSE WHO WORSHIPPED ITS IMAGE. THESE TWO WERE THROWN ALIVE INTO THE LAKE OF FIRE THAT BURNS WITH SUPHUR. (**v21**) AND THE REST WERE SLAIN BY THE SWORD OF HIM WHO SITS UPON THE HORSE, THE SWORD THAT ISSUES FROM HIS MOUTH AND ALL THE BIRDS GORGED WITH THEIR FLESH."

When Christ arrives and judgment begins, these two who gave themselves to Satan, are first to find themselves, cast into the lake of fire. This is eternal damnation where every unrepentant sinner will find himself eventually. The rest were all killed and their eternal souls go to Hades waiting the final resurrection and judgment at the Great White Throne of God. This is found in Chapter 20 verse 11-12 –"Then I saw a great white throne and he who sat upon it from his presence earth and sky fled away, and no place was found for them, and I saw the dead, great and small, standing before the throne, and the books were opened, also another book was opened which is the book of life and the dead were judged by what was written in the books, by what they had done." It is only those whose sins have been forgiven and have their names in the book of life are safe in Gods world to come. So the souls of all those who have accepted the mark of the Beast and worshipped him find themselves in Hades waiting the final judgement at the Great White Throne when God shall put them into eternity either in heaven or hell because he is creating a new beginning. He destroys them by putting them away so righteousness will reign in the world to come forever.

In C L Parker's studies on 'ESCHATOLOGY' he points out, God is a just Judge who will not condemn a man without a hearing, and as millions land themselves in Hades over centuries, living in the remotest parts of the world, they will not be condemned without hearing the gospel. Remember Jesus before his resurrection, preached to the spirits locked in chains, as in Jude verse 6, I ask the question, what did he preached to them? In the Gospels he said, 'if the works Christ performed in Capernaum had been done in Sodom, they would have repented'. C L Parker, I believe was one of the only theologians in the Pentecostal Circle who saw this. It took me about 5 years of studying, to understand him. I have rewritten every scripture, in both his two books, 'Original sin', and 'Seven foundation truths'. No wonder he taught in Oxford University, that is why it took so long, to take it in, as I still take his notes to read from time to time.

REVELATION CHAPTER 20 VERSES 1- 3

GOD'S ANGEL BINDS THE DEFEATED DRAGON FOR A THOUSAND YEARS.

Verse 1 "THEN I SAW AN ANGEL COMING DOWN FROM HEAVEN HOLDING IN HIS HAND THE KEY OF THE BOTTOMLESS PIT, AND A GREAT CHAIN. **(v2)** HE SEIZED THE DRAGON, THAT ANCIENT SERPENT, WHO IS THE DEVIL AND SATAN, AND BOUND HIM FOR A THOUSAND YEARS, **(v3)** AND THREW HIM INTO THE PIT, AND SHUT IT AND SEALED IT OVER HIM THAT HE SHOULD DECEIVE THE NATIONS NO MORE, TILL THE THOUSAND YEARS WERE ENDED, AFTER THAT HE MUST BE LOOSED FOR A LITTLE WHILE."

This follows straight after the judgment of Satan's two associates the beast and the false prophet who were put away for eternity in hell, where the worm dieth not nor is the fire quenched a place of eternal condemnation. But the dragon is only put away for a thousand years at this stage in time, he will be chained in the bottomless pit. This Dragon had tremendous power and authority as a cherub in heaven, remember in the book of Jude, v. 9, when the Angel Michael was contending over the body of Moses, he did not bring a railing accusation against him, but said "The Lord rebuke you". When Satan is cast out of heaven he also loses some of his authority so that an ordinary Angel could bind him and put him away.

Again we are told of a few names he uses, throughout the Bible, one is the Ancient Serpent who brought sin and death in the garden of Eden, Adam and Eve passed down in their seed a weakness in the flesh, so that when Cain came to an age of understanding he was deceived by sin even after God had warned him that sin lieth at the door. But he ignored God and allowed his anger to rise, and then he killed Abel. As Paul said in Roman's 'without the law sin was dead'. Everyone must grow to an age of understanding the law before they become transgressors, for what the law could not do, in that it was weak through the flesh, God sending his own Son in the likeness of sinful flesh and for sin condemned sin in the flesh. As

Christ was tempted at all points as we are yet without sin. So the Grace of our Lord Jesus Christ frees us from the law of sin and death, since Christ rose victorious over all.

I've digressed a little from the verses to C L Parkers teaching on anthropology that took me about 5 years to study. He wrote this and taught it in the Pentecostal Bible College in the early 1930's. So Christ sets free every repentant sinner who cries out in true repentance and also by faith in the resurrection they are justified and made free from the law of sin and death. This is Christ's millennial sign when the world will be free from the temptation of Satan.

REVELATION CHAPTER 20 VERSE 4

CHRIST TRUSTED SAINTS WILL RULE WITH HIM IN HIS MILLENNIAL REIGN

Verse 4 "THEN I SAW THRONES AND SEATED ON THEM WERE THOSE TO WHOM JUDGMENT WAS COMMITTED, ALSO I SAW THE SOULS OF THOSE WHO HAD BEEN BEHEADED FOR THEIR TESTIMONY TO JESUS AND FOR THE WORD OF GOD AND WHO HAD NOT WORSHIPPED THE BEAST OR ITS IMAGE AND HAD NOT RECEIVED ITS MARK ON THEIR FOREHEADS OR THEIR HANDS. THEY CAME TO LIFE AND REIGNED WITH CHRIST A THOUSAND YEARS."

The whole purpose of our Lord is to transform us into Christ's image. Trials and persecution are the way our Lord took, and this is the only way to prove our faithfulness to him. We must grow to maturity. This can only be achieved, by the temptations we pass through as our Lord was tempted at all points as we are, yet without sin.

The greatest test of Jesus, was experiencing the death on the cross, yet even in this his faith never wavered. The death we may have to face is being beheaded for our faith, and not accepting the beast and his mark. There is only one religion which still holds this death penalty of beheading, that is the Moslem faith. We all have witnessed the extremism of this faith which is causing wars and terrorism throughout the world.

This extremism seems to increase towards the end. Praise God, Christ is coming back to reign and all the dead in Christ will be raised to meet our Lord in the air. Paul never feared death; for he said that to be absent form the body is to be present with the Lord. Only our body goes into the ground, our soul and spirit goes into heaven if we are saved.

Our Lord said, "All who are in the graves shall hear the voice of God, and come forth", then those who have, done good, to the resurrection of Life, and it is then, that Body, Soul and Spirit are united forever in heaven.

REVELATION CHAPTER 20 VERSES 5 - 6

OUR LORD DISTINGUISHES THE TWO RESURRECTIONS AND THE TWO DEATHS

Verse 5 “THE REST OF THE DEAD DID NOT COME TO LIFE UNTIL THE THOUSAND YEARS WERE ENDED, THIS IS THE FIRST RESURRECTION (**v6**) BLESSED AND HOLY IS HE WHO SHARES IN THE FIRST RESURRECTION OVER SUCH, THE SECOND DEATH HAS NO POWER, BUT THEY SHALL BE PRIESTS OF GOD AND OF CHRIST AND THEY SHALL REIGN WITH HIM A THOUSAND YEARS.”

There are two resurrections spoken of here, the first comes to establish his rule , and start Christ’s 1,000 years millennial reign over the earth. In the gospel of Matthew chapter 24 verse 31 it says "He will send out his angel with a loud trumpet call and they will gather his elect from the four winds from one end of heaven to the other" If you go back to verse 29 this happens immediately after the tribulation of those days. 1 Thessalonians chapter 4 verses 16-18 reads, “For the Lord himself will descend from heaven with a cry of command with Arch-angels call, and with the sound of the trumpet of God. The dead in Christ will rise first, then we who are alive who are left, shall be caught up together with them in the clouds to meet the Lord in the air; so shall we always be with the Lord."

All scripture regarding the end times, interlink with the book of Revelation, If you think of all who are justified by faith in Christ from Genesis to Revelation there must be billions of saints in this resurrection, yet among these who are sanctified by faith, who were prepared to be martyred rather than bow to the Beast and his image, and receive his mark, are those who are to reign upon the earth in the thousand year reign of Christ. The second resurrection comes at the end of Christ's reign when all the dead left in the grave; the billions who have transgressed Gods Law, and millions who have never heard his law or the gospel of Christ, will be resurrected to be judged as we read and study later in this book at the great white throne of God, when every sinful and ungodly person will be judged , those whose names are not written in the book of life will suffer a second death, when God destroys their bodies, casting them into Hell along with their soul for eternity. This is the only way God can eliminate sin from the earth. Our God believes in the death penalty, for the preservation and protection of the righteous, who are saved forever.

REVELATION CHAPTER 20 VERSES 7 - 8

WHEN SATAN IS RELEASED FROM PRISON HE WARS AGAINST CHRIST'S HOLY CITY.

Verse 7 "WHEN THE THOUSAND YEARS ARE ENDED, SATAN WILL BE LOOSED FROM HIS PRISON"

Verse 8 "AND WILL COME OUT TO DECEIVE THE NATIONS WHICH ARE AT THE FOUR CORNERS OF THE EARTH. THAT IS GOG, AND MAGOG, TO GATHER THEM FOR BATTLE; THEIR NUMBER IS LIKE THE SAND OF THE SEA."

We might ask why did God only put Satan away for a thousand years, was it because he is long suffering and forbearing willing that none should perish, but that all should come to repentance, or was it to test the nations of the world who have lived without sin and wars with Christ for a thousand years. Could they return to Satan's power after peace and righteousness.

One thing we do realise, a thousand years in prison doesn't change Satan's ways; the nations of the world who were allowed to live on earth under Christ's reign, have no guarantee of eternal security. This proves that God wants his sons to have a sanctified life that will not be persuaded by temptation to transgress again, but grow in love, knowledge and faithfulness like God the Father, and God the Son, who was tempted in all points like us, yet without sin.

This was the whole purpose of our Lords coming, to show Gods love and the sacrifice on the cross for our redemption from sin, so that we no longer live to satisfy the desires of the flesh. It does not say how long Satan took to deceive the nations of the world to gather an army against the Lord and his city Jerusalem. It seems easy that so many nations can be persuaded to sin after Christ had ruled them for a thousand years, so our destiny for the future is based on how we grow to be like Jesus, perfect in all our ways, this is the only guarantee to live safe with him forever. Eternal determination to obey God is the only guarantee of eternal security.

REVELATION CHAPTER 20 VERSES 9 - 10

THERE IS NO ETERNAL SECURITY UNTIL SATAN IS BANISHED TO HELL.

Verse 9 "AND THEY MARCHED UP OVER THE BROAD EARTH AND SURROUNDED THE CAMP OF THE SAINT'S AND THE BELOVED CITY; BUT FIRE CAME DOWN FROM HEAVEN AND CONSUMED THEM. (**v10**) AND THE DEVIL WHO HAD DECEIVED THEM WAS THROWN INTO THE LAKE OF FIRE AND SUPHUR WHERE THE BEAST

AND THE FALSE PROPHET WERE, AND THEY WILL BE TORMENTED DAY AND NIGHT FOR EVER AND EVER."

Satan has lived thousands of years even before our creation. He was a covering cherub in God's throne. It was then that he desired to be like God and sin entered his heart, he then deceived a third of the angels in heaven to sin. He didn't even stop at that, for he attacked Adam and Eve and deceived Eve and the inhabitants of the world. Here after he suffered a 1000 years in prison he is unable to be changed. But he comes out to deceive the nations again. So will every person who doesn't repent and believe the gospel of Gods beloved Son. They are unable to be changed. If Gods grace is refused he is left with no alternative but to put sinners away forever in hell. We see here that the Beloved City has been rebuilt after being destroyed 3 times in the past. One might ask, what is Hell? it's the loss of mans body a second time, after he's been to the judgment seat of God, which the next few verses speak of, which God has recorded in their lives on earth, written in verse 12.

There will be millions who have never heard the gospel in the remote places of the world, but God has said in Romans that he has placed the law of Good and evil in every persons heart, so that as the elders of the remotest village sat down to make laws and commandments Gods law would come forth. Every person is responsible for doing right or wrong. This is seen in the story of Lazarus and the rich man, who feasted daily with much food while Lazarus was dying of starvation and ill health, the rich man had no love or compassion and Lazarus died, and went to heaven, both were born in Israel under the law of God, but the rich man broke the Law, by not loving his neighbour as himself. Therefore, he finds his eternal soul in Hades awaiting the second resurrection to the great white throne of God, when the final judgement takes place from the record of his life on earth, in the books written in heaven. For God will not condemn any to hell without a hearing, for he is a just Judge. Man leaves his riches and pleasures behind forever, and leaving his sinful life, which becomes his torment in Hades. His soul cannot die, but he looses his spirit and body, this is the teaching of C L Parker, from 1930, and this is still available from the Pentecostal Bible Shop in Nottingham.

REVELATION CHAPTER 20 VERSES 11 - 15

GOD'S FINAL JUDGMENT ON UNGODLINESS FROM THE BEGINNING OF CREATION.

Verse 11 "THEN I SAW A GREAT WHITE THRONE AND HE WHO SAT UPON IT, FROM HIS PRESENCE EARTH AND SKY FLED AWAY, AND NO PLACE WAS FOUND FOR THEM."

Verse 12 "AND I SAW THE DEAD, GREAT AND SMALL, STANDING BEFORE THE THRONE, THE BOOKS WERE OPENED, ALSO ANOTHER BOOK, WHICH IS THE BOOK OF LIFE. THE DEAD WERE JUDGED BY WHAT WAS WRITTEN IN THE BOOKS, BY WHAT THEY HAD DONE."

Verse 13 "AND THE SEAS GAVE UP THEIR DEAD, DEATH AND HADES GAVE UP THE DEAD IN THEM, AND ALL WERE JUDGED BY WHAT THEY HAD DONE."

Verse 14 "THEN DEATH AND HADES WERE THROWN INTO THE LAKE OF FIRE."

Remember the thousand year reign of our Lord has just finished, we have seen the saints of God resurrected into heaven at the beginning of his reign, This being the first resurrection which he spoke of in verse 6, "Blessed and holy is he who shares in the first resurrection! Over such the second death has no power, but they shall be priests of God and of Christ, and they shall reign with him a thousand years". So billions of saints are resurrected into heaven also a certain number from each tribe of Israel, which I think, reign on the earth with Christ, as found in Chapter 7 verse 4, then also in verses 9 to 11. In Corinthians Chapter 6 verse 3, it says, "Do you not know that we are to judge Angels?" As Christians and saints, we must grow in grace and knowledge, so that we are capable of judging Angels, to accomplish this one must grow in stature like Christ.

In John's Gospel Chapter 5 Verses 28-29 it talks of two resurrections "Do not marvel at this for the hour is coming when all who are in the graves will hear his voice and come forth, those who have done good, to the resurrection of life, and those who have done evil, to the resurrection of judgment." First, is the resurrection of the saints, then a thousand years later comes the resurrection of judgment of the ungodly. If God can place billions of stars in the sky, he can certainly keep an account in the books of heaven of all the ungodly deeds committed in the earth. We also see another book which is the book of life, and unless their names are written in this book they are cast into the lake of fire which is their second death, an eternal place for their souls.

C L Parker brings some very truthful teaching which stirs our minds to think on this judgment, the first is 'have you never heard of a judgment condemning anyone without a hearing?' and standing before God are millions of people throughout history that have lived and died in the remotest parts of the world who have never heard the gospel of the saving grace of Jesus.

How will God judge them, if they have never heard the gospel? Remember in 1 Peter chapter 3 verse 19 it says that while the body of Jesus lay in the tomb, his spirit went and preached to the disobedient spirits, fallen from heaven in Noah's day, when they left heaven desiring the daughters of men, and God locked them away in chains. I personally, believe he preached the saving grace of his gospel, so God will see to it that the world will hear the gospel before they are condemned. Even those in the remotest part of the world who have never heard the gospel Matthew 24 verse 44 and Revelation 14 verse 6.

How can it be more tolerable in the Day of Judgment, for Sodom and Gomorrah, if they had seen the miracles that Capernaum had seen which was written in the Gospel of Matthew Chapter 11 verses 23-24, it says they would have repented if they had seen Christ's miracles. It says also, unless a man repent he will likewise perish, so I believe that some sinners will be saved on judgment day at the Great White Throne. This doctrine is found in the teaching of C L Parkers book on Original sin and Eternal judgment, if you want to understand more.

So our God is a just God and a merciful God, if we never had a chance to hear the gospel during our lifetime on earth. Can a just and righteous God condemn anyone without a hearing, If our Lord preached to spirits in his death, can sinners be restored and their names written in the book of life at this judgment? All judges on earth do not condemn men without a hearing, and whosoever shall call on the Lord in true repentance like the dying thief, who was only a cry away, and so was I, and He saved us both.

Eternal sin can only be eliminated by an eternal banishment to hell, where 'the eternal soul, is, where the Worm dieth no more and the fire is not quenched'. I believe that this fire is when the body is separated from the soul, and all the sinful desires of the flesh, that are unfulfilled causes torment to the soul in eternity.

REVELATION CHAPTER 21 VERSE 1

GOD'S TIME TO RE-CREATE A NEW HEAVEN AND A NEW EARTH

Verse 1 "THEN I SAW A NEW HEAVEN AND A NEW EARTH, FOR THE FIRST HEAVEN AND THE FIRST EARTH HAD PASSED AWAY AND THE SEA WAS NO MORE."

In Genesis one, we see the beginning of the old creation, as we are living in now. Then we read of the fall of Adam and Eve to sin, through the temptation of Satan. The result to mankind was devastating with Cain slaying his brother Abel, then by Genesis six, the whole world had fallen under Satan's power, so that every person's heart was deceitful and desperately wicked and violence filled the earth, leaving God no alternative but to annihilate mankind, only allowing Noah and his family to re-populate the world. So here God starts with a new earth and a new Heaven, in which only those people who have been cleansed through the blood of the Lamb, Gods Son, and have been changed and have partaken of his divine nature and are holy and worthy to live in his new creation.

In making a new creation he does away with the sea, which he had created in his first creation, one might ask why, would he remove the sea? One possibility is that the sea has claimed the lives of so many innocent victims. Remember in Christ's time, on the Sea of Galilee, the apostles were threatened by a storm, and our Lord had to rebuke the wind and the waves, so Satan must be behind certain storms in life that need rebuking.

Also, Paul was in a sea storm as he was being shipped as a prisoner to Rome, but our Lord was gracious and delivered all on board when it was shipwrecked. Paul also spoke in his epistle of being cast into the sea three times and the Lord delivered him, So Jesus is Lord of the seas. God shows that he has no further use for the sea in his new earth.

REVELATION CHAPTER, 21 VERSES 2 - 4

GOD'S NEW HOLY CITY DESCENDS FROM HEAVEN AS A BRIDE.

Verse 2 "AND I SAW THE HOLY CITY, NEW JERUSALEM COMING DOWN OUT OF HEAVEN FROM GOD, PREPARED AS A BRIDE ADORNED FOR HER HUSBAND."

Verse 3 "AND I HEARD A LOUD VOICE FROM THE THRONE SAYING "BEHOLD THE DWELLING OF GOD IS WITH MEN, HE WILL DWELL WITH THEM AND THEY SHALL BE HIS PEOPLE"."

Verse 4 "HE WILL WIPE AWAY EVERY TEAR FROM THEIR EYES AND DEATH SHALL BE NO MORE NEITHER SHALL THERE BE MOURNING NOR CRYING NOR PAIN ANY MORE, FOR THE FORMER THINGS HAVE PASSED AWAY."

In Gods first creation, he made the sun, moon and stars, all for the benefit of mankind. As we circle the sun we have four wonderful seasons, then as the moon circles the earth, we have a perfect day system, every seed he multiplies, thirty, sixty, a hundred fold, so that he feeds the whole earth. What a mighty and wonderful God!

In the new creation he has built a Holy City a New Jerusalem specially prepared in heaven, then, against the laws of nature, he brings it down as a bride for her husband. This city was the dwelling place of God with man, a mansion prepared for millions of Saints of God, who are resurrected to reign on earth, in his new creation.

A new beginning, a new life, eternally with God himself, our past is gone forever, for there is no more weeping, no more death, no more suffering, all the consequences of sin in the old creation have vanished forever.

REVELATION CHAPTER 21 VERSES 5 - 7

ALL CHRISTIANS ARE ASSURED BY GOD'S ETERNAL NAME, ALPHA AND OMEGA.

Verse 5 “AND HE WHO SAT UPON THE THRONE SAID " BEHOLD I MAKE ALL THINGS NEW" ALSO HE SAID "WRITE THIS, FOR THESE WORDS ARE TRUSTWORTHY AND TRUE".”

Verse 6 “AND HE SAID TO ME, "IT IS DONE; I AM ALPHA AND OMEGA, THE BEGINNING AND THE END. TO THE THIRSTY I WILL GIVE FROM THE FOUNTAIN OF WATER OF LIFE WITHOUT PAYMENT".”

Verse 7 “HE WHO CONQUERS SHALL HAVE THIS HERITAGE, AND I WILL BE HIS GOD AND HE SHALL BE MY SON.”

Our Lord is still on the throne as he passes from his old creation to his new creation. In Genesis he filled the earth with life, and he gave life to Adam and Eve, then life to the sea-world then life to the birds of the air, then life to the animal world. In the gospel of John, Chapter 1, 'All things were made by the word of God who is Jesus Christ, who has predestined us before the foundation of the world to be transformed into His image'.

Our Lord is also the Alpha and Omega, the beginning of creation and the end of creation as he is everlasting he makes a new creation and a new city, a New Jerusalem. Then, looking back into Genesis we see a tree of life, which God had to take away because of sin, so that death reigned until Christ the word of God, died and rose from the dead, and justified all believers in him to a new life in his new creation.

Here in his new creation, he has put a river of life, so we are free to drink and live forever, and this, like the tree of life in the Garden of Eden, is a free gift from God. Remember, since accepting Christ into our lives in our old creation we became over-comers to the temptations of Satan, which we faced daily in the old life, this was the only way we could be holy to live forever in the Holy City , New Jerusalem.

REVELATION CHAPTER 21 VERSE 8

A LIFE OF SIN WILL TAKE US INTO ETERNAL DAMNATION IF WE DON'T REPENT.

Verse 8 "BUT AS FOR THE COWARDLY, AND FAITHLESS, THE POLLUTED, AS FOR MURDERERS, FORNICATORS, SORCERERS, IDOLATERS AND ALL LIARS, THEIR LOT SHALL BE IN THE LAKE THAT BURNS WITH FIRE, AND SULPHUR, WHICH IS THE SECOND DEATH."

Every person from the age of understanding, find themselves indulging in these sins and unless they are redeemed from all their sins in this life by the blood of the Lamb, Jesus Christ they are destined to hell, which is for the everlasting soul of man. God destroys his body, which is described here as the second death. If God made a soul to live forever, in a body and then suddenly finds himself alone in Hell and with all these sins which he has committed while on the Earth. We can see this described in the gospels, where it says; "is like a worm that does not die, or the fire quenched."

In the story of the rich man and Lazarus both had the law given to them, but the rich man lived a life for himself, and not for God, and Lazarus must have cried out to the Lord for help. The Lord heard him, and took him to paradise where as the rich man eventually died and went into Hades, and his soul found itself in torment. One might say he was responsible for

Lazarus death, for he broke the second commandment of God for he had no love for his neighbour, and all who do these sins mentioned here, also break God commandments and will find themselves in Hell.

Our Lord continually spoke of the good seed, and the bad seed, being separated at the end on the Day of Judgment and the wheat and the tares separated and the tares burnt up when he spoke of the two resurrections, the good to the resurrection of life, and those who have done evil, to the resurrection of judgment. Again Jesus said "He that believeth in me shall be saved; he that believeth not in the Son of God shall be damned". So Hell is an eternal place, prepared for all unrepentant transgressors of God's laws.

.

REVELATION CHAPTER 21 VERSES 9 - 11

GOD'S GLORIOUS HOLY CITY JERUSALEM REVEALS HIS GLORY ON EARTH.

Verse 9 "THEN CAME ONE OF THE SEVEN ANGELS WHO HAD THE SEVEN BOWLS FULL OF THE SEVEN LAST PLAGUES, AND SPOKE TO ME, SAYING "COME I WILL SHOW YOU THE BRIDE, THE WIFE OF THE LAMB"."

Verse 10 "AND IN THE SPIRIT HE CARRIED ME AWAY TO A GREAT HIGH MOUNTAIN, AND SHOWED ME THE HOLY CITY JERUSALEM, COMING OUT OF HEAVEN FROM GOD, HAVING THE GLORY OF GOD."

Verse 11 "ITS RADIANCE LIKE A RARE JEWEL LIKE JASPER, CLEAR AS CRYSTAL."

The angels are entrusted to reveal what will happen even after the millennial reign of Christ, when they see this glorious city created by God for all his saints on earth. This is a Holy City, and saints are to become holy as he is holy, to live with him in the city. John was to see and witness with this angel this city descending from heaven 1,500 miles square which will cover many Middle-Eastern Countries.

When you see all the stars set in the Universe, you have no difficulty in believing, that we have a great and mighty and a loving God, who creates this City with millions and millions of rooms. So the Saints can live with him forever, in the New Jerusalem which is created in heaven and descends to the Middle-East.

REVELATION CHAPTER 21, VERSES 12-14

HOW OUR LORD'S GLORIOUS CITY EMBRACES THE OLD AND NEW TESTAMENTS

Verse 12 "IT HAD A GREAT HIGH WALL, WITH TWELVE GATES AND AT THE GATES TWELVE ANGELS AND ON THE GATES THE NAMES OF TWELVE TRIBES, OF THE SONS OF ISRAEL, WERE INSCRIBED. (**v13**) INSCRIBED ON EACH ENTRANCE ON THE EAST THREE GATES, ON THE NORTH THREE GATES, ON THE SOUTH THREE GATES AND ON THE WEST THREE GATES. (**v14**) AND THE WALL OF THE CITY HAD TWELVE FOUNDATIONS AND ON THEM THE TWELVE NAMES OF THE TWELVE APOSTLES OF THE LAMB."

The word of the Lord and the promises of the Lord are forever. It says Heaven and earth will pass away, but the word of the Lord, abideth forever. It is written, Abraham believed God, and it was appointed to him for righteousness. God promises he would multiply his seed, as many as the stars of heaven, for the multitudes and the sand on the seashore. Here we have Abraham, Isaac and Jacob's seed, the twelve tribes of the sons of Israel, on each entrance three facing in each direction, east, north, south and west as the same tribes that encamped around the tabernacle in the wilderness. You may ask how these names are engraved at each gate. How did they find favour after selling Joseph and committing sinful acts but all were wonderfully saved when facing Joseph and seeing the mighty hand of God in their deliverance.

As Jesus did, for the woman caught in Adultery, she should have died, but our Lord saved her, and said "Go and sin no more". Saved, like us when we come in repentance. So, they have embraced his promises and they are in the New Jerusalem. Then we see the twelve apostles of the Lamb, placed in the foundations stones of this Holy City. They were entrusted with the glorious gospel that whosoever shall call on the name of the Lord shall be saved. It takes the same faith in the Old Testament as in the New Testament to be saved. As we read in Hebrews Chapter 11, verses 8-10 "By faith Abraham obeyed when he was called to go out to a place which he was to receive as an inheritance, he went out not knowing where he was to go, By faith he sojourned in the land of promise as in a foreign land, living in tents with Isaac and Jacob heirs with him of the same promise. For he looked forward to the city, which has foundation, whose builder and maker is God." This also proves the Bible promises are seen in the New Creation. Looking at the city it will always remind us of his eternal Great love in the past the present, and the future.

REVELATION CHAPTER 21 VERSES 15 - 17

THE VASTNESS OF THE NEW JERUSALEM STRUCTURE REVEALS GOD'S GLORY

Verse 15 "AND HE WHO TALKED WITH ME HAD A MEASURING ROD OF GOLD TO MEASURE THE CITY, AND ITS GATES AND WALLS."

Verse 16 "THIS CITY LIES FOUR SQUARE ITS LENGTH THE SAME AS ITS BREADTH HE MEASURES THE CITY WITH HIS ROD TWELVE

THOUSAND STADIA ITS LENGTH AND BREADTH AND HEIGHT ARE EQUAL."

Verse 17 "HE ALSO MEASURES ITS WALL, A HUNDRED AND FORTY FOUR CUBITS BY A MAN'S MEASURE, THAT IS, AN ANGEL'S."

Never in the past have we heard or seen anything so wonderful and outstanding in the earth as this Holy City, this New Jerusalem. Its size covers 1,500 miles square; when you think of Babylon 500 miles walking distance from Jerusalem and add 3 times to this distance, it would cover many countries in the Middle Eastern world.

It is beyond our comprehension that God's City could house millions of saints who are worthy to live in it. This same Angel had a rod to measure it, When you think of all the capital cities in the world, like London Paris, New York Rome and hundreds more, all could fit into this great heavenly city, New Jerusalem, which has been designed and built in heaven. No wonder the bible says, 'Eye hath not seen, nor ear heard, neither hath it entered into the hearts of men, the things that God hath prepared for those who love him'.

REVELATION CHAPTER 21 VERSES 18 - 21

OUR GOD'S GLORIOUS BEAUTY IS BUILT INTO ITS STRUCTURE

Verse 18 "THE WALL, WAS BUILT OF JASPER, WHILE THE CITY WAS PURE GOLD, CLEAR AS GLASS."

Verse 19 "THE FOUNDATIONS OF THE CITY WERE ADORNED WITH EVERY JEWEL; THE FIRST WAS JASPER, AND THE SECOND SAPPHIRE, THE THIRD AGATE, THE FOURTH EMERALD,"

Verse 20 "THE FIFTH ONYX, THE SIXTH CARNELIAN, THE SEVETH CHRYSOLITE, THE EIGHTH BERYL, THE NINTH TOPAZ, THE TENTH CHRYSOPRASE, THE ELEVENTH JACINTH, THE TWELTH AMETHYST."

Verse 21 "AND THE TWELVE GATES WERE TWELVE PEARLS, EACH OF THE GATES MADE OF A SINGLE PEARL, AND THE STREETS OF THE CITY, WERE PURE GOLD, TRANSPARENT AS GLASS."

In this present world we see wonderful beauty, as seen in the birds and their various colours, we see a few of them in zoo's in our country. Look at the fish of the sea, the multi-colours, thousands of different kinds of them, then look at the flowers, that God created and all the various colours of the food we eat, from the land, the trees, and the sea, all created for our benefit.

But, here we see a City, beyond description in wonder, beauty and grace, created for the Holy Saints of God. Think of the main materials for this City, pure gold, everything is pure gold, and clear as crystal, fifteen hundred miles square, One can hardly imagine walking on streets of pure gold, but, built in to this pure gold is every precious stone mentioned in the text, are there thousands of jewels or millions of jewels ? We will have to wait and see?

This is God's handiwork for those who love him, 'also in my Fathers house are many rooms, I go to prepare a place for you', the Father Son and Holy Ghost, the God-head, are all preparing this Holy City, New Jerusalem, and these three, Father Son and Holy Spirit are working in Christian lives, to be holy people to enjoy our full salvation in our Lord's Eternal City.

REVELATION CHAPTER 21 VERSES 22 - 27

GOD'S GLORY IS THE GLORIOUS LIGHT OF THE CITY WHICH DRAWS WORSHIPPERS.

Verse 22 "AND I SAW NO TEMPLE IN THE CITY, FOR IT'S TEMPLE IS THE LORD GOD ALMIGHTY AND THE LAMB, (**v23**) THE CITY HAS NO NEED OF SUN OR MOON TO SHINE UPON IT, FOR THE GLORY OF GOD IS IT'S LIGHT, AND IT'S LAMP IS THE LAMB. (**v24**) BY ITS LIGHT SHALL THE NATIONS WALK; AND THE KINGS OF THE EARTH SHALL BRING THEIR GLORY INTO IT. (**v25**) AND ITS GATES SHALL NEVER BE SHUT BY DAY, AND THERE SHALL BE NO NIGHT THERE. (**v26**) THEY SHALL BRING INTO IT THE GLORY AND HONOUR OF THE NATIONS. (**v27**) BUT NOTHING UNCLEAN SHALL ENTER IT, NOR ANY ONE WHO PRACTISES ABOMINATION OR FALSEHOOD BUT ONLY THOSE WHO ARE WRITTEN IN THE LAMB'S BOOK OF LIFE."

In every temple build for the Lord to dwell, both the one in the wilderness and then Solomon's temple, no one could enter until the Glory of God filled it first, as though he sanctioned it to be opened by his presence. But here the city is sustained by the continual light of his glory. This proves God lives in this city, which makes this city, the most glorious on the earth. It may be the most glorious city in the Universe. Try to think of its Beauty, pure clear gold with a light greater that the light of the sun and all these millions of jewels, as it is 1,500miles square, all illuminating the world with the beautiful colours from these jewels, fitting into the foundation of the city.

Look at a Jewellers shop window, with a few small lights, and how it catches the eyes of people passing by, then imagine the glory and colour far greater that all colours of the fish in the sea, the birds of the air or the flowers of the earth, as it all concentrated into this great Holy City that He has prepared for eternity.. This light is the light of the world for the saints, not only to live in but also to walk in the light of his word so that we are saints in character and the nations of the world will also be drawn to worship Christ in the city. The door or gates to this city will always be open to those sanctified by the blood of the Lamb of God who gives us this eternal life in the world to come.

No more darkness in God's eternal city. A beacon so all may come to worship, praise and glory in the God of their salvation. Just think, no more sin no more wars or transgression, but the peace that passes all understanding shall reign forever. All those who have transgressed in the former world and never had their sins forgiven or had their names written in the Lambs book of life, will be banished into Hell forever, so that righteousness will rule in the world to come. What a wonderful future God has promised to all those who love him and keep his commandments. Glory to God in the highest. Glory to God in his holy City. Glory to God forever. Amen, Amen, Amen.

REVELATION CHAPTER 22 VERSES 1- 2

THE ETERNAL WATER OF LIFE, FLOWS FROM GOD'S THRONE.

Verse 1 "THEN HE SHOWED ME THE RIVER OF THE WATER OF LIFE, BRIGHT AS CRYSTAL, FLOWING FROM THE THRONE OF GOD, AND OF THE LAMB,"

Verse 2 "THROUGH THE MIDDLE OF THE STREETS OF THE CITY, ALSO, ON EITHER SIDE OF THE RIVER, THE TREE OF LIFE, WITH ITS TWELVE KINDS OF FRUIT, YIELDING ITS FRUIT EACH MONTH; AND THE LEAVES OF THE TREE WERE FOR THE HEALING OF THE NATIONS."

In the beginning of Genesis God placed the tree of life so man could eat and live forever, but through the transgression of Adam and Eve, they were driven from the Garden of Eden, and from the tree of life, and death reigned throughout the world, so because we all transgressed

His laws, and through the Lamb of God who was sacrificed for the world's sin, we are promised eternal life in the world to come.

So here, in the New Creation, New Holy City and from the throne, Christ the Lamb of God, comes the water of life flowing from their throne which produces the fruit of the tree of life, with leaves that are for the healing of the nations, this seems to imply the need for perfection in our bodies, but provision is made to live forever, with our Lord.

In Ezekiel Chapter 47 it speaks of the Millennial Reign of Christ. Ezekiel speaks of another Temple and the water emerging from the threshold of this Temple got deeper and deeper until one could swim in it and finally it ran east and west when the Mount of Olives was split into a great Valley at the Coming of Christ. So the water ran into both the Dead Sea and the Mediterranean Sea (which I spoke about in the 2nd Trumpet on page 39) when the Mediterranean Sea was contaminated by a Nuclear explosion. So the Seas were purified and replenished with fish. Coming back to the New Creation, everyone in it has Eternal life. But the Water of Life coming from the Throne produces trees whose leaves are for the healing of the Nations. I believe these are for those saved at the Great White Throne Judgement.

REVELATION CHAPTER 22 VERSES 3 – 5

DELIVERANCE AND WORSHIP TO FATHER AND SON IN THE NEW HOLY CITY.

Verse 3 "THERE SHALL NO MORE, BE ANYTHING ACCURSED, BUT THE THRONE OF GOD, AND OF THE LAMB, SHALL BE IN IT, AND HIS SERVANTS SHALL WORSHIP HIM."

Verse 4 "THEY SHALL SEE HIS FACE, AND HIS NAME SHALL BE ON THEIR FOREHEADS."

Verse 5 "AND NIGHT SHALL BE NO MORE; THEY NEED NO LIGHT OF LAMP OR SUN, FOR THE LORD GOD WILL BE THEIR LIGHT, AND THEY WILL REIGN FOREVER AND EVER."

In the next world, there will be purified saints from the old world, there will be nothing unclean in his new city, all the nations of the world will come to worship their Lord and God in spiritual truth. Each person who comes to worship will see his face, so those who see him have also been cleansed and purified, for no one can come to God unless he has been cleansed and purified and is Holy as He is holy. There are also servants in attitude as our Lord came to serve, not as a Lord although he was the Lord of Lords, and King of Kings.

All the Angels sent to earth came as ministering Angels sent to the heirs of Salvation so they were servants of God. Remember through the blood of our Lords sacrifice we are made sons, joint heirs with Christ and he has baptised us in his Spirit so we can be led by the Spirit in every situation in life against all the trials of life even if we are afflicted like Job, or have been beaten three times like Paul, for if we suffer with him we will also reign with him, so we are partakers of his divine nature to help us to become like our Lord in character.

If we are to rule Angels in the world to come, we must be also like Daniel, Shadrach, Meshach and Abednego, David, Job, etc. all who have passed through great trials, and persecutions by the same anointing of the Holy Spirit and would rather face death than bow to the idols of this world. Christ reigned in their hearts, as our Lord cried " Let not my will be done, but thy will be done" even unto death on the cross. In Genesis we see God created the sun to be the light of the world and beyond, but in the next world this city has God as its light within the city, and for the whole world.

REVELATION CHAPTER 22 VERSES 6 – 7

GOD'S ANGEL REVEALS TRUTH TO HIS APOSTLE JOHN, CONCERNING THE FUTURE.

Verse 6 “AND HE SAID TO ME "THESE WORDS ARE TRUSTWORTHY AND TRUE, AND THE LORD, THE GOD OF THE SPIRITS OF THE PROPHETS HAS SENT HIS ANGEL TO SHOW HIS SERVANTS WHAT MUST SOON TAKE PLACE",”

Verse 7 "AND BEHOLD I AM COMING SOON, BLESSED IS HE, WHO KEEPS THE WORDS OF THE PROPHECY OF THIS BOOK."

Our Lord ascended into heaven and is interceding on our behalf, He has also been glorified with the same glory as His Father, all power has been given to him, so the book of Revelation is special, in the sense that it is given to us directly through the Lord by his Angel.

All scripture is given by the inspiration of God, as men spoke as they were moved by God. Hebrews Chapter 1, verses 1 and 2, 'In many and various way God spoke of old to our fathers by the prophets, but in these last days he has spoken to us by his Son, who He appointed the heir of all things, through whom also he created the world', and Christ is saying at the end of the book of Revelation "Behold I am coming soon", these words are trustworthy and sure and when all that is written in Revelation concerning the end time is fulfilled then he will come.

We must realise that the words of the prophecy are both trustworthy and true and all these events spoken, must be fulfilled. They were given to us by the glorified Christ, who created the world. When he was living on earth in the flesh he was limited in many ways, as he had to eat, drink, rest and then he died, but now, he is alive for ever more, and not only does his Father know the day and the hour, but the Son does too, and has revealed the truth of end times, the day He comes for us to take us to himself, to those who are looking for his coming.

REVELATION CHAPTER 22 VERSES 8 – 9

THE DANGER OF WORSHIPPING MINISTERS WHO REVEAL GOD'S TRUTH.

Verse 8 "I JOHN AM HE, WHO HEARD AND SAW THESE THINGS, AND WHEN I HEARD, I FELL DOWN TO WORSHIP AT THE FEET OF THE ANGEL WHO SHOWED THEM TO ME;"

Verse 9 "BUT HE SAID TO ME "YOU MUST NOT DO THAT! I AM A FELLOW SERVANT WITH YOU, AND YOUR BRETHREN AND

PROPHETS, AND WITH THOSE WHO KEEP THE WORDS OF THIS BOOK, WORSHIP GOD"."

It is so easy to get carried away by ministers who reveal the truth, or for people in high positions with deep understanding in Gods word. The danger is to fall down in worship or to put them on a higher level. How many Kings and Ministers of the gospel, have been lifted up and have fallen back into a world of sin. Many young men have spoken Gods word from the pulpit and gone back into the world.

The World is full of men who once walked with God, but have fallen back into old sinful ways. Angels are just servants, they are sent from God to minister to the heirs of salvation as servants. I personally believe that all Angels are positioned differently in Heaven, for many have passed through the temptations of Satan as over-comers and their faith has been strengthened by God.

So God can trust his Angels to live close to him and reveal his truth to Apostles and Prophets and also to reprove them and correct them in love, this is the whole purpose of Christ's coming into the world, not just to save us, but to transform us into saints to replenish the heaven and replace Angels who have fallen with Satan, but we must be transformed into Christ's likeness. There is only one God and we should only worship Him, and always remember we are all brethren.

REVELATION CHAPTER 22 VERSES 10 - 15

GOOD AND EVIL ARE IN EXISTENCE UNTIL THE DAY OF THE LORD.

Verse 10 "AND HE SAID TO ME "DO NOT SEAL UP THE WORDS OF THE PROPHECY OF THIS BOOK, FOR THE TIME IS NEAR"."

Verse 11 "LET THE EVILDOERS STILL DO EVIL, THE FILTHY STILL BE FILTHY, AND THE RIGHTEOUS STILL DO RIGHT, AND THE HOLY STILL BE HOLY."

Verse 12 "BEHOLD I AM COMING SOON, BRINGING MY RECOMPENSE TO PAY EVERY ONE FOR WHAT HE HAS DONE."

Verse 13 "I AM THE ALPHA AND OMEGA THE FIRST AND THE LAST THE BEGINNING AND THE END."

Verse 14 "BLESSED ARE THOSE WHO WASH THEIR ROBES, THAT THEY MAY HAVE THE RIGHT TO THE TREE OF LIFE, AND THAT THEY MAY ENTER THE CITY BY THE GATES."

Verse 15 "OUTSIDE ARE DOGS AND SORCERERS AND FORNICATORS AND MURDERERS AND IDOLATERS AND EVERY PERSON WHO LOVES AND PRACTICES FALSEHOOD."

The first thing we read is both good and evil people, are still living together at the coming of the Lord. Our Lord told a parable in Matthew, Chapter 13, verses 24 - 30. 'The kingdom of heaven may be compared to a man who sowed good seed in his field, but while men were sleeping, his enemy came and sowed weeds among the wheat, and went away. So when the plants came up and bore grain, then the weeds appeared also. And the servants of the householder came and said to him, "Sir did you not sow good seed in you field? How then has it weeds?" He said to them, "An enemy has done this." The servants said to him, "Then do you want us to go and gather them?" but he said, "no lest in gathering the weeds you root up the wheat along with them, let them both grow together until the harvest, and at harvest time I will tell the reapers Gather the weeds first, and bind them in bundles to be burned but gather the wheat into barns."

Moving on to verse 36-43, his disciples ask him to explain the parable of the weeds. He answered "He who sows the good seed is the Son of Man. The field is the world, and the good seed means the sons of the Kingdom. The weeds are like the sons of the evil one, and the enemy who sowed them is the Devil. The harvest is the close of the age and the reapers are Angels. Just as the weeds are gathered and burned with fire, so will it be at the close of the age. The Son of Man will send his Angels and they gather out of his Kingdom all causes of sin, and evildoers and throw them into the furnace of fire, there, men will weep and gnash their teeth then the righteous will shine like the sun in the Kingdom of their Father, He who has ears, let him hear". So we see both good seed and bad seed grow together until the day of the harvest, the two reaping are at the same time. If we go to Matthew Chapter 24, verses 29-31 Listen to what he says, 'Immediately after the tribulation of those days, the sun will be darkened and the moon will not give her light, and the stars will fall from heaven, and the powers of the heaven will be shaken, then will appear the sign of the Son of Man in Heaven, and then all tribes of the earth will mourn (bad seed) and they will see the Son of Man coming on the clouds of Heaven with Power and great Glory and he will send his Angels with a trumpet call and they will gather his Elect (good seed) from the four winds from one end of Heaven to the other.'

So this agrees with Christ's Parable perfectly, then going on to Ch.24 v.36 He talks of only his Father as the only one knowing this day, as the Son of God laid aside his glory. In John Ch.1 v.14, 'and the word was made flesh and dwelt among us and we beheld his glory, glory as of the only Son from the Father.' But, after his resurrection and ascension he was glorified to his original status. The Son of God equal with his Father, in power and glory, he then gave us the Book of Revelation which shows every step and sign to his second coming. By going over and re-iterating, some of the Book of Revelation, you can apply it to the end of the age, and the coming of the glorified Christ.

The sixth seal, in Revelation Chapter 6 verse 12 to 17, it says "I looked and behold there was a great earthquake, and the sun became black as sackcloth, the full moon became like blood, and the stars of the sky fell to earth as the fig tree sheds its winter fruit when shaken by a gale, the sky vanished like a scroll that is rolled up , and every mountain and island, was removed from it place, then the kings of the earth and the great men and the generals and the rich and strong, and every one, slave and free hid in the caves, and among the rocks of the mountain, calling to the mountains and rocks, "Fall upon us and hide us from the face of him who is seated on the throne, and the wrath of the Lamb, For the great day of his wrath has come, and who can stand before it ".Then we witness what also is happening on the day of his wrath which is the day the Lamb sets up his throne in the millennium reign with 144,000. 12,000 from each of the 12 tribes of Israel who are to reign on earth.

Then if you go to Chapter 7 verse 9 it also speaks of the rapture of his saints at his coming. "After this I looked and behold, a great multitude which no man could number from every nation from all the tribes and people and tongues standing before the throne and before the Lamb clothed in white robes with palm branches in their hands and crying out with a loud voice "Salvation belongs to our God who sits upon the throne and to the Lamb," and all the Angels stood around the throne and round the elders and the four living creatures and they fell on their faces before the throne and worshipped God". (Good seed) Moving down a few verses to Verse 14 it tells us where these multitudes come from, "and He said to me, these are they, who have come out of great tribulation, they have washed their robes and made them white in the blood of the Lamb. Therefore they are before the throne of God, serving him day and night within the temple." If you read on it tells of the suffering they had to endure in the great tribulation such as, hunger, thirst, and scorching heat.

Then I would like to speak about the devastation which the seven trumpets reveal in the great tribulation as I have written in Chapters 8 to 11, the first trumpets reveal the destruction of a third of the world's vegetation, then a great bomb landing in the sea, and the devastation caused in the sea, then a chemical poisons the rivers and water systems that had a codename 'wormwood' which killed millions of people. Then we see a great alteration in the heavenly creation, the sun, moon, and stars, after this we see the world leader Satan as the Angel of the bottomless pit, and his world army, who killed a third of the population of the world. Then God's two prophets appear in Jerusalem for a three and a half year ministry, after which the Anti-Christ killed them in Jerusalem, and if we go forward to Chapter 11, verses 15-19, the last trumpet is the beginning of Christ's Kingdom, as it is written. 'Then the seventh Angel blew his trumpet, and there were loud voices in Heaven saying, "The Kingdom of the world has become the Kingdom of our Lord and of his Christ. And he shall reign for ever and ever". And the 24 Elders who sit on their thrones before God, fell on their faces and worshipped God saying "We give thanks to thee Lord God Almighty, who art and who was; that thou hast taken thy great power and begun to reign." You can link this revelation with many second coming scriptures. "The Nations raged but thy wrath came, and the time for the dead to be judged," <u>Event 1.</u> For rewarding thy servants the prophets and saints and those who fear thy name both small and great. <u>Event 2.</u> For destroying, the destroyers of the earth.

Here the ungodly are under his wrath and the saints are being rewarded in Heaven. In Chapter's 12 to 14 we see Satan being cast out of heaven and going to attack the Christians in Israel. Failing in this task, he turns to persecute the Christians worldwide. In Chapter 13 we see Satan and his two associates the Beast and False Prophet and all their evil tactics and supernatural powers, trying to convince the world to worship him. In Chapter 14 Verses 14 - 20 speaking of two reapings, first the Son of Man reaping the saints, and another Angel came out of the temple, calling with a loud voice to him who sat upon the cloud, "Put your sickle and reap, for the hour to reap has come, for the Harvest of the earth is fully ripe, and the earth was reaped. (So the good seed was reaped to Heaven, spoken in the parable of the good seed and the bad seed. Then came the reaping of the bad seed, verse 17, and another Angel came out of the temple in heaven, he too had a sharp sickle, then another Angel came out from the Altar, the Angel who had power over fire, and he called with a loud voice to him who had the sharp sickle "Put in your sickle and gather the cluster of the vine of the earth for the grapes are ripe. So the Angel swung his sickle on the earth and threw it into the great Wine press of the wrath of God, and the winepress was trodden outside the city. And the blood flowed from the wine press as high as the horses bridle for one thousand six hundred stadia. The sixth bowl or plague in Chapter 16 was poured out at the Battle of Armageddon when two hundred million were slaughtered and their blood flowed as deep as the horse's bridles. How expositors have been misled on this major issue, I will never fully understand. Because we are dealing with these last verses in the book of Revelations let us return to them and see how they fit into this truth, as seen in Chapter 22 verses 10-15.

This book must not be sealed up, for the words of the prophecy of this book must be kept for our Lord's coming, At his coming he talks of evil-doers, the bad seed, still doing evil, when Christ comes to recompense in judgement the Holy and good seed, who went into Heaven, and the evil bad seed, he will destroy in Hell. He is the Alpha and Omega, the beginning of a new creation wherein dwells righteousness then he reigns forever in a New City and the righteous will take of the tree of life by the river of the water of life. But the evil doers find themselves in hell, for eternity such as sorcerers, fornicators and murderers and Idolaters and every sinful person. There are two events happening on the same day, Our Lords Return, spoken of in Matthew Chapter 24, verses 36 - 39 where it's talking about his coming in Glory and judgment. He says "but on that day and hour, no-one knows, not even the Angels in Heaven nor the Son, but only the father." Jesus said this before he was glorified with the Father again and becoming co-equal in power, glory and wisdom.

The next verse gives us more understanding of the two events just as the book of Revelation makes it very clear, these two events happen on the same day 'As were the days of Noah so it will be at the coming of the Son of Man. For as in the days before the flood they were eating and drinking, marrying and giving in marriage, until the day when Noah entered the Ark, and they did not know until the flood swept them all away, so it will be at the coming of the Son of Man. Two events, Noah was saved on that day, and the ungodly perished. After our Lord was glorified with his Father he gave us all the revelation concerning the day of our Lord, and the events of the Tribulation, when he comes to separate the good seed from the bad.

REVELATION CHAPTER 22 VERSES 16 - 17

OUR LORD WANTS HIS CHURCHES WORLD WIDE TO KNOW THE TRUTH OF HIS REVELATION.

Verse 16 "I JESUS HAVE SENT MY ANGEL TO YOU WITH THIS TESTIMONY FOR THE CHURCHES I AM THE ROOT AND OFFSPRING OF DAVID , THE BRIGHT AND MORNING STAR" **(v17)** THE SPIRIT AND THE BRIDE SAY "COME" AND LET HIM WHO HEARS SAY "COME" AND LET HIM WHO IS THIRSTY COME, LET HIM TAKE THE WATER OF LIFE WITHOUT PRICE."

Our Lord God Almighty, Jesus Christ sent this Angel to John, to write this last Chapter of his first creation and the beginning of his new creation. Before King David was born, before Abraham was born, He was the Alpha and Omega, and He is the Alpha and Omega of the new world, the new creation, the new city Jerusalem. He also was the Son of God, and the Son of Man, for He also was born as a descendant of David and the offspring of David, who offers eternal life to mankind, if we repent of sin, and believe that He died at Calvary, for our sin, which he bore on the cross. He rose again from the grave, and is offering every one the chance to live for ever more in the new Heaven, in this new Jerusalem. This is the love of God that passes all understanding, God wants all to repent, and hear his call to "Come". His Spirit and Bride invite you to come, but the hearers must be doers and come at his call to drink of the water of life freely, Christ's invitation is to all; He is not willing that any should perish but that all come to repentance, for God so loved the world that he gave his only begotten Son, that whosoever believeth in him shall not perish but have everlasting life, for God sent not his Son into the world to condemn the world, but to save it, we must hear his call to "Come."

I would like to testify to my calling into Bible College. I was forty years old and at a meeting in the Town Hall, Bishop Auckland, where in the early 1930's many hundreds were saved and healed as Stephen Jeffries preached 'Christ' and many churches were established in our area, I wanted to do something for God, and I said to the Lord, "If you want me to do some thing in your work, tell me to go into the work, say one word, "Go" or, if you want me to have training in a Bible College, I want you to say "Come". Immediately, someone spoke in tongues, and Idris Parry, Ex-Missionary, who was Pastor at the local Assemblies of God Church, interpreted it. The word was, "I say unto you. Come" My heart jumped as I heard it. At home, at that time, I had 3 children a son who was 18, a daughter that was 10, and a boy of 2 years, I also had another son who was 19 and in Bible College. In the next few weeks, I wanted to be sure that this was God calling. We had arranged to go to A.O.G. General conference, and I wanted confirmation that I was doing the right thing, so I prayed "Lord if you want me to come into Bible college, then call me 3 times, 'Come". So I went to the conference in expectation, In every service I was listening intently to every sermon as the days passed by one after the other. Then in one of the last services, a Minister called Douglas Quy spoke, and the text was one I have here Rev.Ch.22 V.17, I had only been saved 12 years, and never knew there was the word "Come" three times in that same passage of the Bible, although I must have read it a hundred times, again I could hardly believe it, but I wrote for a grant, and it was accepted, I had very little money in the bank. Working at a local factory, I had just finished building a bungalow, which had put me in debt, so I arranged for a bridging loan, for a year, from a Christian bank Manager. God provided for my family and myself, remember I had very little education and had only read a few books beside my Bible, so soon I found myself like a fish out of water, in Bible College. It was after college that I realized why God had taken me there. A new Principal had just taken over, called David Powell, and he was taking us for 'Homiletics and Hermeneutics' i.e. splitting a Chapter into headings and sub-headings, I was taken up with this, and believe the main thing I learnt in College, was in fact 'Homiletics and Hermeneutics'.

On Leaving Bible College, God got me a caretaker's job, with four hours off during the day, my wife had a part-time job so she was out of the house while I was at home those four hours, I was able to study the subject 'eschatology' The Second Coming of Christ, especially Revelation. In 30 years, I believe I have written out, Revelation from Chapter 4 to Chapter.22, five times, and studied it verse by verse. Now, I'm writing it for the last time. I believe anyone who is gifted to preach is able to teach from these notes. Bible Students or seeking Saints are able to improve on my headings and sub-headings if they do a little studying to understand it, as our Lord revealed it to me by his Spirit. Many books have been written on End time, with different theories, yet, the evidence I've written is completely different. I believe this is the only reason why he chose me to study this one subject for 30 years. I'm sure God has not led me as a Christian all this time on one book without bringing forth fruit for my labour, I can only plead "God takes the weak things of the earth, the base things of the earth, the things that are nothing, to confound the mighty."

REVELATION CHAPTER 22 VERSES 18 - 21

THE DANGER OF FALSELY INTERPRETING SCRIPTURE, INVOLVES JUDGMENT.

Verse 18 "I WARN EVERYONE WHO HEARS THE WORDS OF THE PROPHECY OF THIS BOOK, IF ANYONE ADDS TO THEM, GOD WILL ADD TO HIM, THE PLAGUES, DESCRIBED IN THIS BOOK."

Verse 19 "AND IF ANYONE TAKES AWAY FROM THE WORDS OF THIS BOOK, OF THIS PROPHECY, GOD WILL TAKE AWAY HIS SHARE IN THE TREE OF LIFE AND IN THE HOLY CITY, WHICH ARE DESCRIBED IN THIS BOOK."

God is warning all who are writing and giving their views and teachings on this book to be very careful, for the book of Revelation is a prophetic book, and our Lord has revealed these truths of end times. If you remember, it was holy men moved by the gifts of the Holy Spirit, the words of God's wisdom, a word of God's knowledge and all of his other seven gifts that are seen in the Bible. Howard Carter spent several years before writing a book and teaching it in the Bible College, when it first opened in 1930, so only God can move upon us to reveal his truths. To add to God's truth as the Pharisees did, or to take away from his truth, will only bring judgment, so let us reason together for the truth, let us keep humble, meek and lowly, and ever abounding in the love of God.

Verse 20 "HE WHO TESTIFIES TO THESE THINGS SAY, "SURELY I AM COMING SOON" AMEN, COME LORD JESUS.

Verse 21 "THE GRACE OF THE LORD JESUS, BE WITH ALL THE SAINTS, AMEN."

We all know the coming of the Lord is drawing near, His promises are sure, and "Amen" He is coming soon. So let us look up, for our redemption is nigh, the redemption of our bodies, Revelation Chapter 1 verse 1 reads, The revelation of Jesus Christ, which God gave him to show to his servants what must soon take place; and He made it known by sending his Angels to his servant John, verse 2, who bore witness to the Word of God, and to the testimony of Jesus Christ, even to all that he saw, verse 3, Blessed is he who reads aloud the words of the prophecy and blessed are they who hear, and who keep what is written therein, for the time is near. It's the responsibility of every Christian, not only to read it, but to understand it for themselves. I feel positive that this book will benefit all who read it, and are preparing themselves for the coming of the Lord. For He is coming soon, Amen.

Outline of Revelation

I wrote this outline with its headings and sub-headings to help find any verse or chapter, quickly, when teaching or studying the Book of Revelation.

Outline of Revelation Chapter 4

1st Heading
Verse 1 } John the apostle's calling into heaven.

Sub heading
Verse 2 } Apostles and prophets have special anointing of the spirit to reveal Gods truth.

2nd Heading
Verse 3 } John reveals the glory of God's throne.

Sub heading
Verse 4 } Twenty four elders seated on thrones before God.

Sub heading
Verses 4-7 } These elders had greater revelation to reveal to John.

3rd Heading
Verses 5-6 } The supernatural powers and mysteries around God's throne.

Sub heading
Verses 6-7 } The mystery of the crystal sea before Gods throne.

4th Heading
Verses 6-7 } The four living creatures that move with God.

Sub heading
Verses 8-11 } All these creatures have four faces.

Sub heading
Verses 8-11 } Worship of God starts with the living creatures and escalates throughout all heaven.

Outline of Revelation Chapter 5

1st Heading Verse 1	The mystery book held in Father's hand.
2nd Heading Verses 2-3	A universal search for a holy one to open the book.
Sub heading Verse 4	John wept at how sin affected every sphere of God's creation.
Sub heading Verse5	One of the twenty four elders reveals God's Son can open the book.
3rd Heading Verses 6-7	Christ is also the Lamb of God who can take the book in his Father's hand.
4th Heading Verse 8	All heaven explodes in worship to Father and Son's achievement.
Sub heading Verses 9-10	The words of the worship song declare Christ's redemption work on earth.
Sub heading Verses 11-14	The worship gathers momentum throughout heaven.

Outline of Revelation Chapter 6

1st Heading Verses 1-2	How Satan rules the first four nations who ride different coloured horses in the first four seals. The first seal. The white horse.
Sub heading Verses 3-4	The second seal reveals a second evil man. (Riding a red horse)
Sub heading Verses 5-6	The mystery behind the third rider on the black horse.
Sub heading Verses 7-8	How Satan rules these nations and rides the horse. The fourth seal.
2nd Heading Verses 9-10	The souls of saints martyred under God's altar in heaven.
Sub heading Verse 11	Preparing these souls for the next stage - our bodily resurrection.
3rd Heading Verses 12-14	The sixth seal reveals a geographical change both on earth and in heaven.
4th Heading Verses 15-17	The day of Christ's coming is the day of Christ's wrath.

Outline of Revelation Chapter 7

1st Heading
Verses 1-3 — God's angels called for special mission on earth.

Sub heading
Verses 4-8 — Special remnant of Israel sealed to be saved and rule.

2nd Heading
Verse 9 — The resurrection of the saints at the end of the tribulation.

Sub heading
Verses 10-12 — These resurrected saints cry out in praise and worship with the hosts of heaven.

Sub heading
Verses 13-14 — An elder gives understanding to the apostle John concerning the vision of the resurrection saints.

Sub heading
Verses 15-17 — Christ's blessing to these saints in the world to come.

Outline of Revelation Chapter 10

1st Heading Verse 1	Identifying an angelic heavenly ministry
Sub heading Verses 2-4	John was instructed what to do with the book and the thunders.
2nd Heading Verses 5-7	The angel's revelation on worship and the sound of the last trumpet.
Sub heading Verses 8-11	John receives instruction about the book in the angel's hand.

Outline of Revelation Chapter 11

1st Heading
Verses 1-2 — God's instruction to John regarding the temple at Jerusalem.

Sub heading
Verses 3-6 — God's two witnesses reveal that God is still in charge of end time.

Sub heading
Verses 7-9 — God identifies their assassin and allows them to die.

Sub heading
Verses 10-11 — Gods two righteous servants were resurrected before their eyes.

2nd Heading
Verse 13 — God's judgement on Jerusalem proceeding Christ's coming.

Sub heading
Verses 14-15 — God's final trumpet the last trumpet and final woe.

Sub heading
Verses 16-18 — Worship breaks out in heaven as Christ begins his reign on Earth.

4th Heading
Verse 19 — God re-opens his heavenly temple which he had closed.